HAUNTED

CANTERBURY

T0322585

HAUNTED
CANTERBURY

JOHN HIPPISLEY

The History Press

*To my parents and my sister Christina, and the experiences of many
people without whom this book would not exist!*

First published 2009
Reprinted 2013

The History Press
The Mill, Brimscombe Port
Stroud, Gloucestershire, GL5 2QG
www.thehistorypress.co.uk

British Library Cataloguing in Publication Data.
A catalogue record for this book is available from the British Library.

ISBN 978 0 7524 4998 2

Typesetting and origination by The History Press
Printed in Great Britain

CONTENTS

ABOUT THE AUTHOR

John Hippisley is a ghost hunter, journalist and actor, who runs the Canterbury Ghost Tour on Friday and Saturday evenings and also all-inclusive 'ghost evenings' combining a ghost tour with a meal at a local inn (www.greenbard.8m.com).

He has lived in a sixteenth-century house in nearby Harbledown since 1978, which he shares with the ghosts of Victorian children. John saw his first ghost at thirteen, but did not begin actual phantom sleuthing until 1995.

'Canterbury is one of the most haunted places in England, with apparitions all over the city,' he says. 'The Romans left their mark. Then during the Reformation monks and clergy were slaughtered cruelly, as were witches, and finally the Civil War brought more bloodshed.'

'The most interesting ghost I've been investigating is Simon of Sudbury, Archbishop of Canterbury, who appears in Sudbury Tower in Pound Lane. There are lots of child ghosts, who will play with your coat or jacket as you get close to them. I've had more than sixteen paranormal experiences, – not all ghosts, some poltergeists, and some merely psychic feelings.'

Having a responsible tour guide means you'll be safe from disturbing experiences; however, John believes that you should never treat the supernatural with levity, 'Using a Ouija board can be extremely dangerous. I recently investigated a case in a 300 year old Canterbury building where a group of medical students had a terrifying experience doing so. After research, I concluded that the trouble was caused by a young woman who committed suicide there in 1873.'

John stresses that most ghosts are not harmful or malicious; many in

Canterbury are apparently more scared of being seen than we are of seeing them!

'I love the diversity of Canterbury, enjoy seeing the groups of foreign tourists and am always fascinated by the history that oozes from every pore – the feeling that so much has happened here, intoxicates you. The city bristles with the voices of the past. On a quiet summer's evening you can hear the voices of past residents walking alongside you – absolutely idyllic.'

FOREWORD

When a friend of mine recently asked me if I could write a book about Canterbury's ghosts, I thought about it and agreed that I could, then the thought hit me; what about the people whose homes are haunted? What will happen to the value of their homes? Recent research has shown, however, that some homes with a resident spectre can command a higher price than your average non-haunted home, for those who wish to commune with the dead or recently departed.

I have been running the Canterbury Ghost Tour since 1998 and although it is not the longest running of the tours that have sprung up in the UK, it is one of the few to have won both a tourism award and recognition from the Society for Pyschical Research – an organisation known for its scepticism of all things paranormal.

Many writers have been inspired by Canterbury, most notably Christopher Marlowe and Geoffrey Chaucer, although both for different reasons. In Marlowe's case he was born here as the son of a local cobbler who was granted a scholarship to the King's School, still well regarded for its high standards of educational excellence.

Chaucer however was drawn, as countless pilgrims had been, to the shrine of Thomas a Becket. Some observers today claim that, had it not been for that brutal act, then possibly Canterbury may not be here today.

It's fair to say then that I may not have come here either. One murder or more can have a dramatic effect on the local economy - just look at Fred West in Gloucester or Harold Shipman in Hyde.

It is fair to say that ghosts do not exist simply to give us something to be scared of, nor do they haunt only the buildings or locations where they died. In some cases they haunt areas where they were happiest in life.

Let us imagine what it must be like to be a ghost.

Missing the chance of life everlasting in heaven – whatever that may be – we remain in a transitory state of flux, unable to move on, and in most cases we are not aware that we have even died. People seem to readily ignore us and, on the odd occasion, they do stop and look, they run from us as if our appearance frightens them as much as their appearance does us. There is nothing to eat to temper the ravenous appetite that is the bane of our existence, nor is there anything to drink. It is always freezing cold, even if we died in a hot country.

Frankly I am not surprised that ghosts are not very forthcoming. Ghosts deserve our respect and there is no better way of showing it than remaining fearful of their existence.

Ghosts are not restricted to the Christian Church; there are sightings in every country and every religion – even in countries where there is no religion.

During this book I will try to give you my side of a ghost's story. The explanations are based on my own research carried out over the last sixteen years into all the disturbances in the city of Canterbury.

HAUNTED CANTERBURY

The Roman Fish Market

St Margaret's Street: Stand with the old Roman Fish Market building to your rear and look up to the top floor of the building opposite (Waterstone's bookshop).

This building was once a private dwelling in the heart of the city, owned by Robert Martin, a wealthy cotton merchant who had a fleet of ships that collected cotton from Virginia in the early eighteenth century.

The family became haunted by a tragedy on the top floor of the building. In 1864, their children's nanny, Elise de Grunnes (a Belgian-born au pair), was preparing the nursery for the afternoon story-time when she slipped on a piece of fabric dropped by one of her charges and fell three flights of stairs to her untimely death.

When I first visited the building she had been felt on many occasions, but never seen – for then it was a department store selling cotton and woollen fabrics, owned by the descendants of the original owner and the store was still called Martin's.

The top floor was then used as a coffee shop, and later became a teashop which Waterstones took over in the 1990s. Elise was felt rather than seen, mainly in the early afternoons, when she would move the coffee and tea pots in their stands, making them rattle, and would slam the doors to the fire exit at the back of the property.

People who witnessed these events often claimed to have smelled a light perfume in the air, often followed by a sharp drop in ambient temperature. Should you have access to the top floor you too will feel the unnatural coldness in the room even to this day.

However Elise is not the only spectre in the building, for the original structure was built on the site of a Roman bath house, which once stretched across the street toward the Church of St Margaret's.

The Roman Fish Market

Booksellers in the lower-ground floor have felt more unnatural coldness and feelings of oppression whilst standing at the foot of the main staircase. To one side they have opened a panel in the wall, which clearly displays the remains of the bathhouse and hypocaust (under-floor heating used by the Romans).

It is possible that the spectre is that of a Roman centurion or guard to the baths, though how he died and why he remained here is really a mystery. Several of the staff claim that during stocktaking, the top book from a pile of books always goes missing, to mysteriously return after the stock take has been completed. There are also reports that books re-order themselves in the rack by the bath house wall into non-alphabetic order.

One morning one of the newer members of staff arrived to find that something had spelled the letters VI in yellow bound books in the rack by the same bath house wall. Was this the centurion trying to communicate with his legion?

In both of these cases the movement of inanimate objects has been put down to ghosts – although strictly speaking, most people are convinced that the only supernatural occurrence that can move things is a poltergeist.

Greyfriars Chapel and the Franciscan Gardens Behind the Greyfriars Guest House, No. 6 Stour Street

Greyfriars Chapel is the only building now remaining of the first English Franciscan Friary built in 1267, forty-three years after the first Friars settled in Canterbury, during the time of St Francis of Assisi. As one might expect there are regular sightings of the Friary's monastic residents seen in the gardens here. Not all are friendly though, as many were slaughtered here during the Reformation. Services are still held here, and this may ease the pain of past tortures. The river Stour passed underneath the structure and this gives rise to other phenomena – poltergeist activity in the nearby buildings. As you walk though the low archway you will pass a semi-derelict building on your left. It is in this building that recent investigations by various local ghost hunters have witnessed objects being physically lifted from the ground and often flung across the void in the middle, which is mainly earthen. Whilst we know that the Franciscans, along with all religious denominations in the city, were massacred by King Henry VIII's troops, little is known of their final resting place. Activity reported in Church Street, St Gregory's in the Northgate side of the city, suggests that most corpses were simply burned in a pit and the souls of the dead remain in what is now Christchurch University accommodation block. Archaeological examinations there in the 1980's revealed massive burials from that period.

The Guest House itself claims to be haunted by feelings rather than hooded monks. Many guests have reported waking to find themselves freezing cold in an otherwise heated room, or in most cases, the covers have been pulled from their beds. In some cases, unseen hands are felt pressing down the covers, to keep them warm. Another case was more recently reported where a young girl woke to see in a semi-dream state, the red eyes of something, not necessarily human, staring down at her from the ceiling.

County Clothes and Marlowe's Florists

The narrow little shop of Marlowe's Florists was, until 1942, the main entrance to the Fountain Hotel which stood proudly on the site of what is now the Marlowe Arcade.

On a warm summer evening in June 1942 the German Luftwaffe launched an aerial attack on locations mentioned in a pre-war guidebook as being of historical or architectural interest to visitors. It was used as a guide to bombing those locations that would break the spirit of the English.

One of the many casualties that night was the Fountain Hotel, which had stood proud as a defiant symbol of pilgrims since it was first built in October 1323.

County Clothes and Marlowe's Florists

The Old Mill Cottage, Westgate Court Grove, St Dunstan's

The building was hit by an incendiary bomb, and inside the structure were found the remains of 300 men and women who had been celebrating a regimental handover on that very night. Contemporary accounts held that their screams could be heard over the Cathedral bells as they peeled the curfew.

The site was left a bombed-out shell for fifteen years until the early 1960s, when the remaining structure was pulled down to make space for a large car park. It was not until the 1980s that the present structure was finally opened and ironically, the design followed almost exactly that of the original hotel.

So much was the similarity that within days of work starting the builders claimed they felt they were never truly alone on the site. Tools and small objects such as nails and screws would often be seen to move of their own accord. Even as the scaffolding was being removed, the scaffolders – not normally spooked by anything – claimed to have heard ghostly footsteps following them along the boards, but never on the ladders.

When completed, the upstairs rooms were on the same level as the hotel's old great ballroom, where all the souls had been lost in the past. Here in the rooms of what is now HMV have been heard the sounds of crashing chandeliers and the faint muffled sounds of many running footsteps.

As recently as June 2007, one of the staff at HMV evacuated the building because he could smell a pungent odour of wood-smoke towards the rear of the structure – the same spot where the main fire had started all those years before.

The Old Mill Cottage, Westgate Court Grove, St Dunstan's

Should you chance upon this house during the day, you may be forgiven for thinking what an ideal location it has, close to the city centre and beside a beautiful river, with outstanding views of the Westgate towers and the gardens opposite.

But as the sun sets, the interior takes on a very different feeling. Visiting the house with a friend one dark November evening in the 1980s, I became aware that we were not alone that day.

I turned to my friend and asked if he had heard something downstairs which sounded like a burglar. Saying he had heard it too, we both made our way downstairs, pausing on the bend of the stair for fear of being seen by the intruder. As we both looked, we saw a shadowy figure at the foot of the stairs who appeared to be bending down to pull some form of handle or latch from the floor.

Although we could not see clearly, we both had the same thought – a trap door to a forgotten cellar – which seemed to make some kind of muddled sense at the time. We turned to go back upstairs but something held us there –

whether it was fear or simply apprehension, try as we might we were effectively frozen to the spot. My friend later mentioned that he felt very cold as soon as he saw this man.

The Westgate Towers

The Westgate of Canterbury has been standing guard over the city since it was rebuilt following the Peasants' Revolt in 1381. The original structure was torched during Watt Tyler's rampage through Kent while gathering support for his campaign to rid England of a new tax.

Built of Kentish rag stone, it offers commanding views of the city and has an excellent museum inside, showing some of the torture techniques used during its grisly past as the town prison.

The Westgate does have a few resident spirits; quite recently one has been seen at ground level crossing the old iron bridge by a passer-by. The spectre in this case may well be a man brought to justice here in the 1880s. During this period a condemned man was habitually walked across this iron bridge and led to the condemned cell in the Westgate.

One night whilst working in the tower, a council worker was just about to leave for the night when he heard what he later described as the sound of a body being dragged down the stone steps on the right side of the tower. Petrified, he decided to head for the main staircase but, as he did so, he found the door had been bolted and locked. Later he also recalled that the temperature surrounding the door was icy cold, and then he heard the sound of running footsteps on the floor above – the roof level.

It sounded like three or four people as the sounds suddenly got louder, and they appeared to descend the stairwell toward his level. Try as he might, he was unable to move the bolt – then, just as he was about to lose all hope of ever getting out, the bolt freed and he scrambled down to the safety of the outside world, his heart pounding in his chest.

Since that night no one has spent any time alone after dark in the tower, and the Council have assured me that people are not allowed to work on their own in there any more.

Sudbury Tower, Pound Lane

A little further down Pound Lane – which is named after the gaol cells that now form part of Kent Music School – toward the Northgate, you will see the square tower in the old wall. This is Sudbury Tower, named after Archbishop

Above and left The Westgate Towers

Simon of Sudbury, who was Archbishop of Canterbury during the Peasants' Revolt in 1381. His untimely death is well documented, but what is unclear is why his spirit haunts the tower which now bears his name.

Simon of Sudbury, one time Archbishop of Canterbury, was born in Sudbury, Suffolk, of middle-class parents. His date of birth is unknown but he died in London, on 14 June 1381.

After studying law in Paris, he proceeded to Rome, where he became chaplain to Pope Innocent VI, and was sent to England as a papal nuncio to Edward III in 1356. In 1361, after being Chancellor of Salisbury, Sudbury was made Bishop of London. While he assisted John of Gaunt over negotiations with France in 1372-73, complaints were made that his cathedral in London was being neglected. To silence his critics, Sudbury enriched the town of his birth by building and endowing a collegiate church on the site of his father's old house.

Sudbury succeeded Langham as Archbishop of Canterbury in 1375, and his friendship with John of Gaunt and the Lancastrian party at once brought him into opposition with Courtenay, Bishop of London, and William of Wykeham, Bishop of Winchester.

Sudbury was an amiable but not a strong man and John of Gaunt's support of Wyclif made him reluctant to proceed against the latter for heresy. Nevertheless, Courtenay's pressure forced Wyclif to be summoned before the Bishops in 1377. But Wyclif, still not under a formal charge of heresy, had Lancaster and the influence of the Court at his back, and escaped condemnation.

Archbishop Sudbury became Lord Chancellor in 1380, on the resignation of Scrope, and his acceptance of this high office cost him his life a year later during the great peasant uprisings.

On 11 June 1381, as the peasants marched on the capital, Sudbury was with Richard II and his ministers in the Tower of London. On 14 June, while Richard was in conference with Watt Tyler at Mile End, agreeing to the peasants' demands, a mob invaded the Tower crying, 'Where is the traitor to the kingdom? Where is the spoiler of the commons?'

'Neither a traitor, nor despoiler am I, but thy Archbishop,' came the reply. In vain the Archbishop warned the mob that heavy punishment would follow his death; the peasants' hatred of those they judged responsible for the Poll Tax left no room in their hearts for mercy. The Archbishop was dragged from his chamber to Tower Hill, and there, after many blows, his head was struck off – to be placed on London Bridge, according to the savage custom of the time.

A few days later, the rising quelled, Sudbury's head was taken down, and together with his body, removed to Canterbury for burial. It was said that Sudbury, when Bishop of London, had discouraged pilgrimages to the shrine of St Thomas at Canterbury; he was known to be an ally of John of Lancaster, and

Sudbury Tower,
Pound Lane

he had imprisoned John Ball, the peasant leader, as his predecessors had done, at Maidstone. But his position as Lord Chancellor was the real cause of Sudbury's violent death. Nevertheless, there were many who loved the mild and gentle Archbishop, and who counted him as a martyr.

During the 1920s Mr Charles Denne was living in this tower, with its resident ghost. Mr Denne's experiences started one evening after he had retired to bed when he heard someone knocking at his bedroom door. There were three distinct knocks, and then the door, although bolted, opened. According to Mr Denne, the figure that stood before him was as solid and as substantial as he was, although wearing very old fashioned clothes.

Mr Denne claimed at the time he was not afraid, as a feeling of a strong air of friendliness emanated from the man. Getting up from his bed, Mr Denne made his guest welcome by offering his outstretched hand to the stranger. As he did so, the tall dignified gentleman with his 'greying square-cut beard' bowed gracefully three times and disappeared.

Thereafter Mr Denne often felt the presence of the ghost and was regularly aware of a pair of hands tucking him into bed. Simon of Sudbury must, therefore, be one of those rare spirits that appear aware of his surroundings, and even able to touch things in the physical world.

No. 36 St Margaret's Street

Here, some eight months ago, several medical students lived and studied on the first and second floors. It's a perfect location in many ways – an off-licence below, a pub within staggering distance, close to the hospital, and lots of retail therapy within easy reach!

One night, following a session in the pub, the students returned here in the early hours and full of confidence, decided to make a Ouija board to contact the dead in their semi-drunken stupor.

Without a board to hand they decided to make one, taking some old cardboard and drawing a circle with the letters of the alphabet, and then the words north, east, south and west and the numbers 1 to 10 around the outside. As a finishing touch they cut out the signs of the zodiac from the Daily Mail.

They took their board to the kitchen on the top floor at the back, and used a kitchen tumbler as their makeshift communicator. Within seconds of lighting a tea light candle and touching the tumbler with their little fingers, they had made some contact.

It is fair to say that using an Ouija board at any time can be very dangerous, but in a building like this, which had been a pub for over 300 years before it became an off-licence, this was risky by any stretch of the imagination.

They asked in a bold voice, 'Is there anybody there?' The glass was jerked towards the YES, and then, according to one of the students whom I later interviewed at length, they got a strange feeling of unhappiness and misfortune, and the lights in the landing flickered and then went out, and the candle flame flickered before flaring up.

They felt sure this was a good sign, and proceeded to ask for a name. The reply was 'Abigail'. No one in the room was called Abigail and none of the students knew anyone of that name, so they pressed on.

'When were you born?' The reply was '1846'. 'When did you die?' '1873' – so she or it was twenty-seven. 'How did you die?' The answer here came as a shock to the students, 'Joshua knows how!' A Joshua who lived with them in the house was away in London that night, and was studying oncology at the local hospital. It did not make any sense. 'Did she die of cancer?' They asked again, and the reply was just as strange, 'David knows the place!'.

David was one of the students, and was getting nervous for, during his first weeks in the house, he had felt the presence of something on the stairs, but he had never told anyone else about the feeling for fear of ridicule. His housemates looked towards him for an explanation, but he could not give one.

Then the glass leapt forward again and spelled out the name of a person who had visited them just that morning. 'Peter Wilkes was here this morning and last Monday,' it read. This meant that whoever was in contact had been watching them for some time. The candle flared up again and then expired, plunging the four students into panic and darkness.

David picked up the board and threw it out of the window, onto the flat roof below. The others, feeling that what they had already experienced was reason enough to feel unhappy, left the room and headed for their own bedrooms. Each locked their door to prevent entry by an unseen force.

David claimed that he then slept relatively soundly for an hour or two, but was woken by the feeling of something sitting on his bed, a heavy man of some kind. In the darkness he wriggled out from under the covers and felt his way down the bed but could not find anyone else in the room. Getting back into bed he pinched himself to confirm he was awake and again felt something pressing hard down on the bed. Thinking this was his imagination, he opened his eyes to find that the kitchen mirror, usually located at the top of the stairwell, was now floating above his head, and his reflection seemed clouded. Reaching around the mirror to see if it was being held up by a wire, he saw the face of an old gnarled woman staring blindly back at him. The face made him scream in terror, waking not only his colleagues but also causing the mirror to shatter, covering him in shards of broken glass. For over a minute his fellow students tried in vain to open the locked door, before using a fire extinguisher to break the door down. By this time poor David had lost over a pint of blood.

Being medically trained, they knew exactly what to do; they called an ambulance and tried to stem the bleeding. David was taken to Kent & Canterbury Hospital, and then transferred to East Grinstead Hospital for skin grafts to his face and chest.

A week after the incident I was called in to investigate the alleged paranormal attack. Prior to going to the property I did my own research and discovered that during the summer of 1873 a young woman, Abigail Peterson, committed suicide on these premises.

According to the local newspaper archives there was some suggestion that her husband, at that time the landlord of what was then the Crown Inn, had taken to beating his wife under the statute known as the 'rule of thumb' which stated that a man could beat his wife with a stick no wider than his thumb.

The story was that Abigail took her own life, following an unsuccessful attempt the previous year, when she had stood on a stool in the top room and attempted to hang herself, only managing to pull the ceiling down. In retaliation, her husband beat her to within an inch of her life.

The following year she was more successful. This time she tied a rope off at the top of the stair well while at the other end she had pre-tied a noose. Placing this over her head, she perched herself on the banister and jumped down the stairwell, pulling her husband's straight razor across her throat as she fell. The downward force was enough to rip her head from her shoulders, and the headless corpse landed on the first bend of the stairs. Her husband, returning from his duties in the pub downstairs at 11 p.m., tripped over the body of his headless wife on the stairs and beat her in anger, assuming her to be drunk or asleep.

Then feeling remorse, he bent down to kiss her. Repulsed by the taste of her blood on his lips, he fled the scene and was soon after arrested for the murder of his long suffering wife.

He was taken to the Pound Lane police station where, during the night, the frightened man took his own life. Ironically he would have been hung anyway, had he been found guilty of her murder.

I brought with me a psychic friend to perform a blessing prayer here and during this short service one of the students from Christchurch University who accompanied us found that, as we neared the top of the stairwell, she felt something stroke the side of her cheek, and brush her hair.

The Little Spirit Boy, Arnet House, Hawks Lane

Let us move on to Arnet House, now a language school, but once where two Georgian houses overlooked a rose garden. The gardens are now a car park, but it was the inside of the structure that led me to investigate here some eight years ago.

During refurbishment to the top floors, workers found small objects moving of their own accord. Most will know that normally means poltergeist activity, so I conducted a number of simple experiments here to establish if this was simply hearsay or something more sinister.

A simple experiment which you can try at home if you suspect there may be a poltergeist in your house is to place a small object, preferably a pen or pencil, under a piece of glass, on a piece of coloured paper with a numbered grid printed on it. In a loud voice ask the spirit to move the object. It may not do it whilst you watch, but if you come back within an hour, it will have moved – how much will depend on your spirit and how much you believe.

The Little Spirit Boy, Arnet House, Hawks Lane

Another idea is to open all the internal doors on the floor where you think there is a spirit. Then place a small make-up mirror on the back of each door. When you close the front door to the property, if there is any spiritual activity then all the doors will slam shut at the same time. I do not know why this works but it does!

In this case at Arnet House there was activity, and quite a bit of it. I called upon my colleague Graham Rowells to help; he is a defrocked Catholic priest who always helps me out at short notice.

He and I went through the 'reaching out process' – whereby you call for the spirit to make itself visible. This is not always recommended as it has its drawbacks.

Here we were lucky. It revealed itself as a small spirit boy, 'Peter', who had been walled up in the attic sometime in the late 1790s, for a crime which he could not reveal. Perhaps he had done nothing wrong, as is so often the case, but he could not make himself heard in the new rooms as they were being refurbished.

Tiny Tim's Tea Rooms, No. 34 St Margaret's Street

In Canterbury there is not quite a ghost around every corner, although St Margaret's Street does have the reputation for being the most haunted street in England, with around twenty-seven sightings a year.

I entered the Geoffrey House, now known as Tiny Tim's Tea Rooms, one evening in 1991. I had been investigating strange appearances and sounds in the building for some months. My colleagues had said that it was all in my mind, but as I entered the building that night it was clear there was more to this feeling than just my imagination.

My fellow investigator Graham Rowells had spent several months in the Cathedral Archive looking at the history of the building and its association with the paranormal. Whilst I was sceptical, I was eager to prove things one way or the other. Following the discovery in the attic space of the corpses of four children, Graham had agreed, after much pressure, to accompany me in this investigation. The bodies had been discovered after a fire in the Geoffrey House, once a Chinese restaurant and located in the heart of old Canterbury. The owner of the restaurant had died in the fire and since then strange occurrences had taken place, including the sounds of running footsteps on the main stairs and the sounds of laughing children in the upstairs room. There was also an unhappy and unnerving atmosphere in the building, which surrounded those that entered. The unusual sounds on the stairwell always seemed to stop abruptly when one's foot was placed on the first tread. Was this an urban legend or did this really happen? This was to be the basis of our investigations on that evening.

Examination of the corpses revealed that they had all died of cholera; a water-borne disease rife in the Middle Ages, and the post mortem also revealed that their shrouds contained hand-written parchments of the Fifth Psalm, written in Latin and clasped in their hands. Carbon-dating had also placed their time of death to within ten years of 1415. The shrouds were hand-stitched and the final stitch was placed through the nostril, signifying a strong link with the seafaring history of the property.

Experiments on the woodwork also revealed that a number of other childrens' deaths had occurred around the same time as these, namely

Tiny Tim's Tea Rooms,
No. 34 St Margaret's Street

commemorative inscriptions on the back of medieval wood-panelling which had been revealed following the fire. Ringlets of children's hair and silver-covered teeth were also found in the brickwork surrounding the main Elizabethan fireplace on the first floor.

We decided that spending the night in the property was the only way to test the myth. As I settled in for the night I zipped my sleeping bag up to my chin to keep out the biting cold, and the candle by me flickered as if caught by some unseen gust of wind. I looked in the direction of the draught but could not see anything, and concentrated again on the candle flame, stretching my legs out in front of me and resting my back against the cold hard wall of the room.

It was now that I heard an altogether different sound, of children singing faintly, almost whispering, a tune. It was like listening to children in a distant playground, where the tune has not been heard for a long time, and I remember the words I heard to this day – 'Al mi candles breden bricther candal lichter faw al nighter'.

At the time I did not understand the language, but have since discovered it was traditionally a medieval song sung over children dying of plague or ague, 'Those children that see this light by their bed will not in the morning, for they will be with the Lord'.

Hardly cheering, but it suggested that these faint voices I heard were those of the children whose corpses had been found in the attic. As I listened the sound was repeated, fainter than before, and then there was total silence. I then felt a weight forming over my outstretched legs, which reminded me of my old headmaster at boarding school years before sitting on my bed telling me, 'There there, there, young lad, that was just a dream…'. Terrified by the feeling and the memory, I zipped the sleeping bag over my head so I could concentrate on my heartbeat and breathing and calm myself.

Then as the weight dissipated, a scream rang out in the darkness. It sounded like Graham had injured himself, so I ran for the door, not a good move if you happen to be in a sleeping bag which is zipped over your head. I stumbled forward and hit the floor, feeling as if I was being attacked by unseen hands from all angles. Try as I might I was unable to get my balance. Then the realization that I did not know in which direction the door was hit me. As I bounced from wall to wall I tried to unzip myself, eventually falling through the door at speed.

Stumbling downstairs I fell into Graham, who, equally scared by the faint singing and drop in temperature, was frantically murmuring the Last Rites in Latin as he ran up the stairs to find me. Meeting me on the landing he reached for his rosary beads, which he had tied around his neck, and I could see he was desperate to leave the building as he wrenched them from his throat, half strangling himself in the process. The beads broke and he then slipped backwards down the stairs on the loose beads on the floor.

Gathering our wits about us, we regrouped and left the building, seeking a whisky to calm our nerves. We must have missed some horrendous paranormal event, for the next morning the door on the top floor had been blown from its hinges by some immense force, there was blood dripping from the walls, a huge wooden cross lay abandoned on the stair carpet and rosary beads were strewn all over several floors.

St Margaret's Church, St Margaret's Street

St Margaret's Church was founded in 1228 on the orders of Peter des Roches, then Bishop of Winchester. Later in the 1850s the church was rebuilt with a new tower. This church was all but destroyed in 1942 during the Baedeker raids, when most of Canterbury and the surrounding area were targeted by German bombers.

The church was then given over to the Deaf Foundation in 1958. By the 1970s it was abandoned again and left to the mercy of two vandals who attacked this church on 29 October 1973.

Using a sledgehammer, they smashed through the doors and once inside they found a large stone slab on the floor. Beyond it lay the fourteenth-century effigy of Sir Geoffrey Newman, who had built much of St Margaret's Street around 1317, which showed him reclining with a naval ship at his feet and the lion of England at his head. Reading the inscription and looking at all the gold leaf around the stone slab, it seems the vandals decided there must be treasure in the vault below. As no one had challenged them, they proceeded to stand on the stone slab whilst hitting it with their sledgehammer. As they struck a second blow the thin stone broke and they fell some fifty feet down into the darkness below, a very long drop.

They were not then aware that the church had been built on the site of a Roman limestone quarry, and was later used as a chapel and wine vault dedicated to the god Bacchus. When the Romans left the city, residents used the vault as a dumping ground for corpses. Even as late as the English Civil War, the vault was filled with the dead from the city's many outbreaks of plague.

The vandals might have died a long death trapped underground, but eventually the local police came to investigate. Rather than jumping into the pit, they used the spiral staircase entrance to gain access, and the two young men were taken to the local hospital and treated for broken ribs, a broken pelvis and two broken legs each. Sadly during their time in the pit they had also ingested small pox bacteria. Their fate is unknown.

The City Fish Bar

On the outside of this building we find a grotesque face of an old man staring at us from high in the rafters. It is the face of Jack in the Green, the pagan god of the trees, the husband of Mother Nature, and the guardian of the underworld.

It also signifies that at some point in its life this structure was the home of an alleged witch. I say this because records show that it was carved in 1190, less than twenty years after the martyrdom and subsequent canonization of Thomas

St Margaret's
Church,
St Margaret's
Street

a Becket of Canterbury, when England was wholly Christian and paganism
had been outlawed. It was during this time of fear and the persecution of
the Muslims during the Second and Third Crusades that witchcraft was first
'diagnosed' amongst many a local woman in the city of Canterbury and the
surrounding areas.

Nowadays we feel secure that witchcraft is not something to be feared but
celebrated, with books by J K Rowling and teenagers desperate to emulate her
hero, Harry. But back in the twelfth century life was different and there was a
very real chance that banishment from the church guaranteed you a place in
eternal hell.

It was during this time then, that a Miss Goodchild lived with her brother,
a fishmonger, on these premises. She was interested in the pagan 'Wicca-

The City Fish Bar, St Margaret's Street

craft' and what it had to offer, for under the pagan religion you could marry for only a year and re-marry every Midsummer's Eve at a place called Kits Coty on Bluebell Hill, near Maidstone. As a pagan you did not have to pay a tithe, or 10 per cent of your wealth, to the church. In an effort to secure their tithes from parishioners, the church ruled that witches – followers of the 'Wicca-craft' –were in fact paying their tithe to the devil and as devil worshippers could be tried for heresy. Heretics in those days were burned alive 'to die as God had intended' but, prior to their execution, alleged witches had to be tested to prove 'beyond any reasonable doubt' that they were indeed witches.

Becket and his predecessors had written various treatises on extracting 'confessions' from witches, often based on advice from the Papal Courts that aimed to rid the world of all non-Christian religions. As a result, with the might of the church on their side, so to speak, their theories on the correct ways to test for witches were straight forward, as follows...

Accuse the 'witch' in front of a large crowd of her peers, which was normally best done on market day. She will usually deny that she is a witch and, if you accuse her three times and she denies it three times then this is the first proof.

The next stage is to take the witch into custody and then publicly test her for witchcraft. This included poking the witch with a witch's pricket, basically a stick with a hidden trigger and a retractable needle. This was used to demonstrate that the witch was in league with the Devil. It was said that where the Devil suckled her blood, he had placed a witch's nipple; thus if you poked a needle on the nipple the witch would not feel it. This was demonstrated first on a local girl with the needle extended. The girl would scream in pain as she was pricked by the sharp needle point, but when testing the witch, the needle was retracted, and her non-reaction then proved to the crowd that she was indeed a witch.

Next the witch was weighed against a bible. If she weighed more than the bible she was a witch, but then of course, even the heaviest bibles would weigh less than a fully-grown woman.

Then there was the flying trial, when the accused was taken to the church towers of St Martin's, St Peters or St Mildred's in Canterbury and flung from the top to see how well they could fly. In most cases they flew really well for the first ninety feet, but safe landings were a problem. Those that died in the trials were buried in consecrated ground with an apology from the church.

Then there was the floating or swimming trial. What better way to test her ability to defy gravity than to ask her if she could swim? If she said yes, they would ask her to confirm this by sticking her thumbs up, then crossing her hands over one another, then bending down to touch her toes. At this point they would nail her thumbs to her feet and ask her again, can you swim?

Still in denial, she would be thrown from the King's Bridge into the then much deeper river Stour to meet her fate. If she drowned she was innocent and the water had forgiven her, but if she swam – and some tried by ripping their own thumbs from their feet - then they were taken for the final trial.

This involved being taken to the Wincheap Green in Canterbury, close to where the Wincheap roundabout is today. Upon this Green stood a giant burnt oak tree, and the witch was tied to the tree and then, to prevent any chance of complaint or of confession, her throat was nailed to the trunk. The blood pouring from her wound was traditionally staunched using 'St Katherine's muslin' – twelve gunpowder charges wrapped in twists of muslin and tied tightly around the neck. A small fire was then set at the witch's feet and she was often rubbed all over with tallow, to increase the burn. As the flames took hold, the crowd would hear the spitting and hissing of the witch as her skin cracked off in the heat and the bodily fluids of the legs cooked. Even today we still hiss at the villain in pantomimes – so nothing has changed.

The Pilgrims' Hospital

Just opposite Lloyds Bank we find Hotel Chocolat which occupies the building once known as the Rose Hotel, where many have seen the ghostly figure of the Monk Hospitaler, or Carmelite monk to you and me! These monks originally stayed in what was once the Pilgrims' Hospital – not a hospital for the sick but derived from the French word 'hosp-it-al-ite', where welcome friendship was offered to strangers and travellers. Here in this building the pilgrims making their weary way to Canterbury were offered free accommodation, often sleeping up to 300 to a chamber on rush matting infested with fleas and with lice crawling over the floors. Some contemporary reports suggested there were enough lice to form the shape of your body during sleep and that the stench of pilgrims could be smelt outside the city walls.

In the 1960s, after several ghostly 'sightings' at the Rose Hotel, a serious operation to exorcise the premises was undertaken by the well-known ghost hunter Canon Ingram-Hill, who promised to remove the ghostly curse which was then preventing the successful sale of the hotel to a new owner. The results were a little more surprising than even he could have predicted, as Ingram-Hill set a trap to encourage the 'ghostly monk' to follow him to the cellars.

The 'spectre' was trapped by nothing more than a locked door in the cellars beneath the building. The 'ghost' was indeed wearing a Carmelite robe, but he had in his possession a number of pieces of jewellery, which he had stolen from hotel guests. This was no ordinary ghost, of course, but a living, breathing man, and it later emerged that ever since the Napoleonic Wars, generations of the same family had robbed hotel guests using their specialist knowledge, passed from father to son, of the underground tunnels that linked the Cathedral to all the hotels and pubs of Canterbury. Some of the tunnels had caved in during the war, but many had remained unknown for centuries.

The police were called and the 'spectre' admitted the thefts and also asked for 180 other robberies to be taken into consideration. He was jailed and released in 1987, but by then the Rose Hotel was long closed and there have been no further sightings of this macabre monk.

The Pilgrim's
Hospital,
St Margaret's
Street

Mercery Lane

Mercery Lane, which leads directly to the Cathedral Gate, is named after the French Protestant traders who arrived here in the later part of the seventeenth century to escape persecution at home. Canterbury Cathedral still holds a French language service in their honour every Sunday if you fancy an unusual day out.

The French traders sold their wares from under the overhanging frontages of the shops in this lane where so many of our English kings and queens have passed over the centuries on their way into the Cathedral, from Henry II and Henry VIII to our own Elizabeth II. Just on the corner of what was once called

Mercery Lane

the 'Chequers of the Hope', is a carving prepared for the royal visit of Henry VIII to the Cathedral, but during the English Civil War Cromwell's troops 'rearranged' the carving into the Lion of England that you see today.

Mercery Lane was also once the site of a large hotel which, according to the Cathedral archives, had 500 rooms arranged around a central courtyard, with up to ten people sleeping in each room. As a consequence, every day the chambermaids would throw all the 'piss-pot-de-poi' from the upper floors out onto the lane as the sun came up around five in the morning, just as the market traders prepared their stalls, all the time shouting the universal old French warning 'Gar Day Loo' (gardez-l'eau)!

Old Boots Store, The Parade

Old Boots Store

There are also some strange carvings above the door here, a sign to a medieval pilgrim that there is sin within. For this was the mark of a house of ill-repute, a bawdy house, where the local girls would help you on your journey to hell...

The Butter Market

Many years ago dairy produce was sold here, but it was also known as the Bull Stake Market. Here they tied up bulls and baited them before slaughtering them in the street, dragging the carcasses to Slaughter Man's Alley (now

The Butter Market

sadly vanished) and thence into Butchery Lane where the meat was sold, still steaming.

The Christchurch Gate

The Cathedral is haunted, as you might expect. Several people have seen chanting monks in the cloister, and most recently a new security guard came upon a party of what he thought were school boys dressed as monks in the cloister. When he challenged them they refused initially to speak, but then they said in unison 'We are to the Scriptorium!'

Satisfied by their response, he continued his journey and commented on the event to his supervisor, who replied in shock 'But all the schoolboys are in bed by this time of night and the Scriptorium burned to the ground in 1100, when eighty monks perished!'

The Christchurch Gate,
Butter Market

The Sun Hotel

The Sun Hotel and Tea Rooms, founded (according to the sign) in 1503, were made famous by the Victorian novelist Charles Dickens, who stayed there in 1841. During his visit he claimed that the spirit of a young girl, 'just seventeen years old and ripe as an orchard in August', visited him on most evenings.

There had been reports of hauntings here before Dickens' visit, many dating from the 1600s, and many eighteenth-century visitors reported that a young girl would enter and tuck the guests in before stroking the side of their cheek, and then departing for the next room.

Legend held that she was the ghost of young Ellen Bean, a cook at Canterbury Cathedral who disappeared one night in 1523. This is quite possible, since at that time the building was the quarters for unmarried staff working at the Cathedral and the adjoining Priory of St Saviour's. Ellen Bean worked as a cook for the Friar of St Saviour's, cooking in what is now the Dean's Palace close to Dark Entry.

The Sun Hotel, Sun Street

The Friar was an amiable man and appreciated her cooking; often claiming that 'Nell could make a feast out of some old boots'. She was flattered that he took to calling her by her nickname, Nelly Cook, but it seems likely that his fellow monks felt jealous he should have a pretty young thing like Nell all to himself.

One Whitsun, the Friar's niece, Annie, arrived from France. His brother was off seeking his fortune on the high seas, so it was the Friar's Christian duty to look after the secular and spiritual needs of his niece during her father's absence. So she came to live in the household.

Nell was surprised at her master's generosity towards the girl, for whilst it was right to show visiting relatives a degree of hospitality, to treat every day as a feast day seemed to Nell a little excessive. Her suspicions were further aroused when she noticed the looks that were exchanged across the dining table most evenings, and the way the Friar kissed his niece. The situation continued unchecked for some three weeks, before an increasingly jealous Nell decided to act.

Each night the young niece would go to her chambers at the top of the house, and the Friar would go to his on the lower floor. But Nell felt all was not as it should be. So one morning she made her way to the niece's bedchamber and placed the fire tongs under the covers. The next day she went back to the room and discovered that the tongs were still there unmoved. Nell surmised that either the young girl was sleeping very uncomfortably or she was definitely sleeping elsewhere. That night she crept to her master's bed chamber, for she could hear what sounded like an unseen assassin trying to choke the Friar in his slumbers. As Nell peered through the keyhole she saw the Friar and Annie together in the room.

Nell decided to visit her friend the apothecary round the corner, and that evening she served her master and his hungry little niece two large slices of game, pie laced with a special wine. The next morning a party of monks called at the Friary to find out why the Friar had not been at prayers as usual earlier in the day. Searching the house, they found the bodies of the master and his young niece lying stone dead in the same incestuous bed, two crusts of a game pie lying between them. To avoid a scandal the monks hastily buried the bodies in the undercroft, and Nell Cook was never seen again!

Well, not alive at any rate. Some three centuries later, in 1849, three stonemasons were called to the foot of the staircase in the Sun Hotel to repair a loose flagstone. On lifting the stone, they felt a cold violent blast of air round their ankles and saw in a shallow chamber no more than six inches deep, the huddled remains of a young girl. Who else could it be but Nell Cook?

Miller's Field

Miller's Field is now one of Canterbury's many car parks, but until 1936 one of the city's biggest flour mills stood where the McCarthy & Stone residential complex now stands. The land under the nearby car park was then a field used to store goods for delivery by river to the Port of Sandwich and thence on to London and beyond.

Now however, the river Stour has silted up and all that remains of the field is the small stretch of grass to one side. It is in this field late at night, after the pubs have closed and the traffic is quiet, that several local residents have claimed to have seen the spiritual apparition of a man in a white smock with a flat grey cap (then a miller's 'uniform') walking soulfully around near the roadside.

The Miller's Arms Public House

The great flour mill that once stood here was destroyed by fire in 1936, but it was not until many years later, in his deathbed confession, that a carpenter confirmed the original cause of the devastating fire.

The carpenter had been sent to the mill in 1936 to replace a loose floorboard, but at the time he had just completed his apprenticeship and had little experience. Unwittingly, he fixed the loose board in place with an iron nail.

Now you may not know this but flour in a confined environment can be explosive and highly combustible. All mills up until that time had therefore been constructed mainly of wood to prevent the danger of ignition, and most workers would wear wooden soled shoes or 'clogs', much as the Dutch did.

By the 1930s people in the UK had taken to wearing heel protectors on their shoes called 'Blakey's', which were made of iron and would stop heels wearing

Miller's Field, The Causeway

down on the streets of any town. However, put a Blakey next to an iron nail and strike the two together and you get a spark. It was this spark that caused the 1936 explosion that destroyed the mill, burning it to the ground in less than four hours.

Until 1964 it was thought that the fire was caused by an arsonist, but nothing was ever proved. So the question still remains; is the ghost that of someone killed in 1947 or a much earlier miller who also perished on the same spot? We may never know!

There is, however, another story associated with this old mill. Nicholas Mason was a hard-working and hard-drinking cobbler who lived next door to the mill with his wife. On most nights Mrs Mason would lie in wait behind the front door, clobbering 'the drunken old sot' as hard as she could as he returned inebriated from the pub. But old Nicholas had a trick or two up his sleeve to avoid a beating. He would creep through the back door and sneak into bed, snoring loudly and pretending he had been in bed for hours, crafty old cobbler.

One night, Nicholas went drinking in the Miller's Arms with a friend, and the two of them began to talk on the subject of ghosts, ghouls and hobgoblins. Soon Nicholas sat, whisky in hand, shaking as if with ague as his friend told

The Miller's Arms Public House, Mill Lane

him tales of murdered men, and long dead misers revealing to the living where they had buried their treasure. Then all of a sudden the clock struck ten; and up jumped Nicholas remembering how he had told his wife he would be back in time for supper at eight. Nicholas' only hope to avoid a severe beating was to do his old trick of sneaking in the back door and dashing up the stairs.

Tonight though, his wife, who had got wise to his tricks, was waiting behind the door for him, and as he clambered up the stairs to bed she walloped him with such force it was lucky she did not kill him, and poor Nicholas sloped off to bed, his tail well and truly between his legs.

However, all the tales he had heard that night seemed to haunt him, and he was unable to get any sleep. It was as though thinking of the dead had summoned them up, for all at once Nicholas felt like someone or something was at the foot of his bed watching him. He sat bolt upright in his bed and stared blankly at the ghastly apparition that stood before him.

In front of him was a giant, almost skeletal, figure – wrapped in a white shroud which floated around him as if blown by some unseen wind. Its hair was matted and jet black and, as Chaucer would have said of his Pardoner; 'It hung down lifeless like a hank of flax'.

The Parrot Inn, Church Lane, St Radigund's

The creature stretched out his bony hand and beckoned Nicholas with an outstretched finger to follow and the now petrified Nicholas decided it was better to follow the figure than face its wrath.

Grabbing his cobbler's bodkin for protection, he followed the beckoning figure, his heart thumping hard in his chest. The ghostly figure appeared to know just where it was going, gliding down the stairs effortlessly, then moving swiftly toward the closed door at the foot of the stairwell which, although recently bolted shut by his wife, then flew open as if on command.

Nicholas nearly fell as he dashed after the ghastly figure, which turned and headed across the bridge toward the old mill and toward the now paved area on the opposite side of the river. The sinister shadow seemed to glisten in the moonlight, and as Nicholas drew nearer it stopped short of the river.

The sound of the rushing water, the cawing of a crow and the scream of a fox sent shivers through Nicholas and did nothing to calm his fears. The figure then stretched out his bony arm and pointed to a rusted iron ring set in the flagstones.

At that moment a cock crowed and Nicholas found himself alone in the cold morning air, the figure having vanished. Fearful that he would not remember the spot in daylight, he thrust his bodkin hard into the ground next to the spot marked by the figure.

Suddenly a scream rang out, and he saw his wife running out of their house clutching her behind, from which protruded his bodkin. For years afterwards, when Nicholas's neighbours talked of ghosts, they still thought about poor old Nicholas and his wife…

The Parrot Inn

The building, now known as the Parrot Inn, was converted into three cottages in the 1870s. In those days one house was called The Cock Pub. There was a private cottage in the middle and on the other side was another pub called The Parrot. The building had been used for many things over the years, but by 1871 it lay empty and decrepit.

A city architect decided there was room to convert the old pubs into cottages to house the local populace, and during this conversion there is documentary evidence that strange occurrences happened.

The first was soon after the building work commenced, when one of the carpenters working on the conversion would often spend nights in the building in order to get an early start on the work. The first thing he noticed was that his tools kept disappearing. His saw – pretty important to a carpenter – mysteriously disappeared from the main staircase (which is still in situ) and

Above and left St Radigund's Church and Alleyway

after an exhaustive search he found it above what is now the kitchens, in what was then the attic space. Was this simply the carpenter's absent-mindedness or something more sinister? The more sceptical of you may plump for the former, but the occurrences did not stop there.

One night soon after the building was finished, the new residents claimed to have been woken by a grey cloaked phantom tearing down the stairs shouting in Latin. That makes some sense as the history of the building confirms it was once the meeting rooms for monks from St Radigund's Church, which is still located next door. Some nights later a similar occurrence took place. This time however, residents saw an eyeless nun surrounded by some kind of blue haze and wearing a tight white wimple, standing silently at the foot of their bed.

Nothing else strange happened for over a year, and then the owner's sister and new husband were staying here on their honeymoon night. Her husband awoke, claiming that he felt a cold wind blowing through the room. When he investigated he found all the windows were firmly shut, yet there was still a stiff breeze in the building. As he watched he saw the shadowy figure of a man dressed in a grey. Cloaked like a monk, his head covered by a cowl, the figure entered through the closed window, which had once been a doorway. It then passed directly through the bed in which his wife lay, eyes wide with fear, and continued through to what are now the kitchens of the restaurant.

St Radigund's Church and Alleyway

Many modern day residents in the area have felt strange auras as they walk down this alleyway toward the Borough. Many claim to experience a suffocating feeling and say that they feel unseen eyes are watching them. Many others have told me of having felt physically pushed toward the road late at night.

The church is now used by the King's School Canterbury, and in the 1940s was converted into a restaurant for the British Army. Several of those who worked on the restoration project in the 1970s also claimed to experience unhappy feelings while working in the church.

One of the men, a plumber, said that he regularly felt he was being watched, and claimed that late one night, whilst working alone, he heard the main church door slam closed. Worried that someone had broken in, he dropped his tools and dashed to the main door. It was firmly bolted shut, and his bag, which he had left by the door, was unmoved. No sooner had he turned his back than he heard the door of the room in which he had been working also slam shut behind him. Rather cautiously he approached the door, and as he did so he clearly saw through the frosted glass the shadow of something walking towards the sinks where he had left his tools. Whether this was simply a case of his

No. 12 Blackfriars Street

The Mint Yard Gate

imagination playing tricks or not, he made a hasty exit, leaving his tools in the bag by the door and heading round to the pub next door.

He returned the next morning to find that his tools and the bag had been moved into the main area of the church. The hammer was balanced on its end, close to the door, as if placed there on purpose by some unseen hand. The plumber has since told me that other tradesmen working in there at the same time had very similar experiences.

No. 12 Blackfriars Street

On Saturday 8 September 1705, Mrs Bargrave of No.12 Blackfriars Street, Canterbury received a visit from her close and dear friend, Mrs Veal of Dover. Their conversation, it seems, was largely of religious matters, but they also talked about Mrs Veal's brother who resided in London.

Mrs Veal was particularly anxious that Mrs Bargrave should relay certain information to her brother about where some gold coins were kept in her house in Dover. Mrs Veal then said rather mysteriously; 'Although it seems unimportant now, you will see the reason for it in the hereafter'.

Mrs Veal then left hurriedly, commenting that she had a long journey to go on two days later. The only curious thing is that Mrs Veal's death was recorded on Friday 7 September 1705, the day before she had called on Mrs Bargrave.

She had been taken ill on the previous Wednesday, and was already in her coffin on the day she visited Mrs Bargrave. Indeed parish records in Dover confirm that Mrs Veal was interred on the Monday 10 September, the day she said she was going on a long journey. Was this a crisis apparition? We may never know.

The Mint Yard Gate

The Borough gate is now one of the main entrances to King's School Canterbury, but it was once the entrance to the rear of the Archbishop's Palace. On 29 December, the anniversary of the murder of Thomas a Becket inside the Cathedral, several people have claimed to hear the mighty clatter of horses' hooves on cobblestones dashing through the Mint Yard Gate, and out in to Palace Street.

So brutal and heinous was Becket's murder by the King's knights that perhaps their memory is somehow embedded into the very fabric of the buildings through which they rode that night...

The Old King's School Shop – Sir John Boys' House

The Old King's School Shop – Sir John Boys' House

This building was, as the name suggests, the old King's School tuck shop, but its history stretches back much further. It was originally constructed by the Lord High Chancellor, Sir John Boys (who was also Constable of Dover Castle and the other Cinque Ports), for Charles I. As one may expect in such an old household, it contains many secrets, not least why the building appears to list so dramatically in a quaintly English way.

In recent years it has been used as a gallery but sadly now (at the time of writing) remains empty and forlorn – a shadow of its former self.

Early one Wednesday evening in December 1987, staff working late in the shop were startled to hear heavy footsteps on the floors above, in a part of the building designated as stock rooms full of uniforms and shirts, which were cluttered and very hard to move around in. Rather tentatively one of the staff members made their way up the narrow twisting stairwell to the first floor where she could feel a cold wind blowing through the room towards her. Worried that someone had inadvertently left the window open she cautiously entered. She claimed later that she felt something pushing her into the room and, feeling unnerved, she turned tail and fled down the stairs, only returning the next morning when the light was better.

As she approached this time she felt the same cold wind, but she knew the window was not open, as she had earlier checked from the outside. Turning to go back downstairs, she saw to her horror a woman standing not three feet away, dressed in a bright red silk dress with fur on the cuffs, and a wide silk collar. The vision's hair was silky and seemed to be floating around her face. The employee stood motionless, transfixed for nearly a minute, scared beyond speech and not a little intrigued. At the back of her mind, however, was the thought that this slender vision could not have been responsible for the heavy footfalls.

The apparition seemed to be aware of its surroundings as it turned and slipped down the stairs and vanished halfway down, as witnessed by the staff member.

The Old Synagogue, King Street

The Old Synagogue in King Street is reminiscent of the great temple of the Egyptians at Karnack. The columns seems to have been hewn from desert sand, although they are more likely to be carved from Bath sandstone, purchased especially for the Jewish congregation which worshipped here in the 1790s when the Synagogue was first constructed.

Since that time it has been taken over by King's School Canterbury as a musical recital room. The acoustics appear to be perfect, and often passers-by hear school pupils rehearsing in the early evening.

Some years ago a local resident passed the gates at the front of the street, and heard the sound of Hebrew chanting. Several of the King's School boys say they have also felt an unwelcome feeling as they entered, but nothing truly malevolent.

The Flemish House, Palace Street

This house was recently converted into a shop specializing in model toys and games but used to be an antique shop selling all manner of objects – some perhaps with a haunted past. Three years ago when the building was being

The Old
Synagogue,
King Street

refurbished, a wall was being knocked down to make way for an en-suite bathroom on the top floor.

As the wall was removed, small silver-covered objects were found in the rubble. The builder, thinking he was onto a rich find, picked them up eagerly, but on closer inspection he realised they were teeth, human teeth, but covered in a fine layer of silver leaf.

No sooner had he placed them in his pocket than he felt what he described as a ghostly wind blowing through the closed front window. He also later recalled that around the same time he put his saw down on the window sill and never saw it again. Concerned that it had dropped out of the open window facing the street, he searched high and low, but never discovered it.

The Flemish House, Palace Street

That is until about three months ago, when a gardener working in the garden at the back of the shop was uprooting an old tree stump and found the saw embedded deep in the wood. The gardener had heard the tale of the lost saw and identified it at once, since the initials of the carpenter and his company name and postcode were upon it.

The tree had been there for at least 100 years, so how the saw came to be buried so deep remains a mystery.

The current incumbents of the shop claim to have smelt pipe tobacco as they climb the stairs to the first floor, and many others have felt unseen hands pushing them to one side of the stairs as they descend, but no apparitions have been seen to date. Is it possible then that whatever haunts this place has lost the

Conquest House, Palace Street

ability to materialise and has to make do with pushing people whilst he puffs on his pipe?

Conquest House, Palace Street

Here we find the oldest house in the city, built for a man called Odo in 1066, hence the name Conquest House. With its long and illustrious past, Conquest House is reputed to be where the knights responsible for Becket's murder lay in wait. The seventeenth-century façade hides the original building which at the time of writing is an antique shop. Back in 2006 the *Most Haunted* television team visited and Derrick Acorah has filmed in here. I have not felt anything sinister here but if the garden is open you will find the remains of the stable block where the knights kept their horses.

The Archbishop's Old Palace, Palace Street

Now part of the King's School, Canterbury, on the day of Thomas a Becket's murder the Old Palace was where the knights gathered prior to launching their fatal attack in the Cathedral.

The Archbishop's Old Palace, Palace Street

The ancient children's nursery-rhyme 'round and round the mulberry bush on a cold and frosty morning' ensured that future generations remembered what happened on 29 December 1170, if only in doggerel. Legend has it that on a cold and frosty morning in bleak mid-winter, the four knights; Reginald Fitz Urse, Hue de Moreville, Richard Le Breton and William de Tracy rode their horses around and around the mulberry bush, 'screaming oaths that tore Christ's blessed body limb from limb', and vowing revenge on Becket for slandering their King by excommunicating the bishops of London, York and Lincoln.

Of all the four knights, it is Reginald Fitz Urse who is most often seen in the cavernous hall of the Old Palace on the anniversary of the murder. No one seems sure how he met his death, so why he would haunt the area remains a mystery, but perhaps he is still doing penance for the murder.

The last sighting was reported to me over two years ago by a security guard, sadly retired now. He was locking up the hall doors one night, having done his sweep of the building when he caught a glimpse of a medieval knight out of the corner of his eye. Later the guard described the figure as being dressed in a knight's tabard and with a sword in his hands, and spoke of how the knight dashed passed him toward the street entrance – perhaps to go back to Conquest House?

He said later that he was terrified not by the spectre but by the feeling of horror that appeared to surround the apparition, an almost palpable fear and loathing. So just take care should you be in the Old Palace on 29 December.

The Poor Priest of St Alphaege's Cottage, Palace Street

Who was the old priest who has haunted this house for so many years? This pretty structure, so often photographed by passers-by, seems an idyllic spot. People who have seen him say this is a 'type two' ghost – unaware of his surroundings and unable to communicate. The only people to have interacted with him say that he stands soulfully at the door to the main front bedroom and seems to look toward the window. Few, however, have seen his face clearly so it is difficult to ascertain what, or perhaps who, he is looking at.

I knew one of the residents here who was the father of a school friend; he often remarked that he could feel the ghostly priest before he could see him, but luckily for the house's current owners no one has seen him for a number of years.

The Flemish Cottages in Turn-Again Lane

The Huguenots, as previously mentioned, left behind many remnants of their traditions, and these houses are some of the best examples in Kent of their distinctive style of architecture. The upper storeys of these cottages have lots of windows, which allowed the extra light needed by the Huguenots' looms to weave high quality fabrics. There is also an expression in common usage, 'spinster', which comes from the Huguenot word 'spinessteres', meaning an unmarried daughter who would spin the raw silk night and day.

The modern owners of these houses have often remarked on the sounds of rapping and tapping in the attic spaces and on the second floors. Are these the Huguenots welcoming the new people to their home? Perhaps they too have happy memories of their time in the city.

The Poor Priest of St Alphaege's Cottage, Palace Street

The Flemish Cottages in Turn-Again Lane

These cottages stand on an unusually named street, on the route down to the river Stour used for centuries by the city's washerwomen. This was still a much used thoroughfare in the period when the Huguenots built these houses, but in the 1890s the street was blocked by a demolished building, and it took so long to clear the rubble that the lane became known locally as Turn-Again Lane. In the early 1970s much of the street was rebuilt.

Mary Tourtel's Birthplace, No. 53 Palace Street

The famous Rupert Bear, that small red-jacketed bear synonymous with the prime years of the Daily Express, was created by Mary Tourtel, who was born in this little house. The story of the little bear that lived in Nutwood has been read by countless generations of children and adults alike, but the woman behind the bear seems largely forgotten. Mary Tourtel was an artist who studied at the Thomas Sydney Cooper College in Canterbury, named after another celebrated local artist of the Victorian period.

Mary's house is now situated above a jeweller's shop, and several people have seen a shadowy figure, both here and in the Chaucer Hotel in Ivy Lane, of an old woman stooping over the bed, by the front window. On the staircase

Mary Tourtel's Birthplace, No. 53 Palace Street

people have felt unseen hands push them down the stairs, and most recently after Hallowe'en, there were several reports of rapping and tapping sounds from the outside of the top windows.

The Old Mayflower Inn – Upper Chamber, No. 59 Palace Street

Many visitors to Canterbury in need of refreshment happen upon this little café with its smoothies and drinks. Few, however, know of its haunted past or of its links with the Pilgrim Fathers. The sign high on the outside wall gives the passer-by a clue, but to find out more I suggest you read the history of the building for yourself.

Robert Cushman, born in Kent about 1580, was the son of a local grocer and one of the leaders of the Puritan revolt against the Catholic King James VI, which led to many Protestants leaving England for good. Labelled non-Conformists and troublemakers by the authorities, warrants for the Puritan ringleaders were circulated to every port in the land, making it near impossible for them to secure a safe passage to the New World. Robert Cushman, meanwhile, hit upon the idea of hiring a boat called the *Mayflower* from this place, then an inn, in the heart of Canterbury, then a city sympathetic to the Protestant cause. Cushman, along with Deacon John Carver, was instrumental in helping other rebellious Protestants escape to Holland, where he joined them several years later in Leyden. He then became a leading member of the Protestant community in Leyden, and took a deep interest in the idea of settling a new English colony across the sea.

In 1617 he was sent with Deacon Carver to London to negotiate with the Virginia Company, which had been granted by Royal Decree all the territory between boundaries 200 miles north and 200 miles south of Point Comfort in the New World, now the USA. Cushman and Carver asked the Virginia Company for permission to settle on their lands, and also applied to King James to grant them liberty of conscience there. The King, however, would only grant them permission to settle, and refused to issue a charter under his seal, though he promised not to molest them.

In 1619 Cushman returned to England with Elder Brewster to plead once more with the King. This time a patent was obtained in which the king granted toleration for their form of religion so long as they remained faithful subjects. Cushman and Carver then came to England to collect subscriptions, make purchases, and prepare for the voyage. Together they chartered the *Mayflower* and, while Carver was busy with the ship at Southampton, Cushman, at the solicitation of the Merchant Adventurers, altered the agreement on his own responsibility, abandoning the two days a week for their private affairs that had been reserved to the colonists in the original contract.

Robert Cushman had by now been named the assistant governor of the new territory but when the *Mayflower* sailed on 6 September 1620, he remained behind to act as their financial agent in England and to send them supplies. In 1621 he published a pamphlet on 'Emigration to America,' urging the advantages of that country for settlement, and in July he sailed for New England on the *Fortune*, taking with him his only son, Thomas, and arriving on 21 November.

He returned to Europe to manage the business of the colonists there, leaving his son in the care of Governor Bradford and his family. Then, on

The Old Mayflower Inn – Upper Chamber,
No. 59 Palace Street

13 December 1621, he sailed for England, and during the voyage he was captured and plundered by the French. Taken to France, he was released after two weeks of detention. On his arrival in England he published an eloquent vindication of the colonial enterprise, and an appeal for Christian missions to be sent to 'civilise' the North American Indians.

In 1623, with Edward Winslow, he obtained from Lord Sheffield a grant of territory on Cape Ann, where a new band of Puritans made the first permanent settlement within the limits of the Massachusetts Bay colony. His son, Thomas, married Mary, third daughter of Isaac Allerton, in about 1635. Always the confidential friend of Governor Bradford, Thomas Cushman became ruling elder of the church on the death of Brewster in 1649. Thomas died in Plymouth, Massachusetts on 11 December 1692 but his wife Mary survived him, and was the last survivor of the *Mayflower* passengers, dying in 1699 at the age of ninety years. Had Mr Cushman not hired the boat in Canterbury then the history of America may have been very different!

Surprisingly the ghostly presence seen by many in the upper chamber of the building is not that of Robert Cushman but of a later seafarer. Dressed in a nineteenth-century style seaman's black and white striped jersey, he stands solemnly on guard as people make their way to the toilets on the first floor. He is often not seen immediately but his presence is sensed, as people come down the stairs and smell the musty odour of his stale pipe tobacco. Many say the old gentleman has a strange air of friendliness about him; and although he does not seem aware of them, they are very aware of him.

There is also a phantom cat in the building which is never seen but whose cries are often heard from the private rooms above the café. People assume that the owner has locked her cat in the upstairs room, only to discover when they enquire that she has no pet cat but only her son's goldfish.

The Archbishop's Stable Block, Behind No. 59 Palace Street

If the gate is open to this well-hidden side alley, take a stroll down to find the old Archbishop's stable block. Inside you will find the stonemasons' workshop. As with many old buildings like the Cathedral, the stonemasons do a sterling job maintaining the masonry and keeping a centuries-old building sound, but as we already know, not every building in the city is as it seems. Indeed one of the masons here recounted the following tale to me.

On a cold December morning in 1986, one Andrew Ball passed through these same gates on his way to work at the masons' shop. As he entered, he saw a young boy standing with his back to the gateway. Dressed in a tweed jacket which appeared tightly buttoned at the front, the boy had on a cloth cap and what appeared to Andrew to be plus-fours or grey trousers, tucked into long black socks, and polished black shoes. Assuming he was lost, Andrew approached and put out his hand to touch the boy on the shoulder to attract his attention. As he was about to touch the child's shoulder, Andrew felt a cold blast of air on his own shoulder and turned away, and when he turned back the child was nowhere to be seen. Concerned that the child might have dashed into the masons' shop, Andrew ran in after him. The other masons already inside looked as if they had literally 'seen a ghost', indeed one old chap (close to retirement) was ashen faced and his hands were shaking.

Some months later, Andrew was attending the old chap's retirement party. During the party the conversation turned to ghosts seen in the masons' shop and the party giver recounted to Andrew a very similar vision, of the same young boy in the same clothes on the very same spot. Andrew was struck by the clarity with which the old man described him, but was even more intrigued by the fact that the vision being described had been seen in 1946, when the old man himself was then an apprentice. The old man also said that back then he too had heard similar stories from his older colleagues, suggesting that this tweed-jacketed little boy was a regular sighting over past decades.

The Archbishop's Stable
Block, behind No. 59
Palace Street

No one who has seen this ghost has been able to pinpoint the age of the child or explain the reason for his appearance, but the fact that it has been seen by so many generations would suggest his demise was no later than the nineteenth century. Just be careful as you walk down the alley that you too do not feel that cold wind on your neck!

The Fire at Sun Street Hotel

With its exposed beams and intricate brickwork, the Sun Hotel is a regular photographic study for many a visitor to the city, and this building truly seems to call out from the past. But it was not always like this.

When I first arrived in the city in the mid-1980s it was, like so many other historic structures in Canterbury, covered in white Victorian stucco. We can see from the plaque high on the wall by the first floor window that Charles Dickens stayed here, although by the same token he seems to have stayed everywhere in Kent and London. In the decades following Dickens' stays here the inn changed tone slightly, becoming known as a 'house of loose morals and even easier virtues'. By 1910 it had quite a reputation for 'helping men further along the road to hell'.

The Fire at Sun Street Hotel, Sun Street

In 1865 a horrific fire ripped through this ancient structure. The local fire wardens provided support as best they could, but the building had no fire insurance so there was little anyone could have done to save it. The fire started on the far side of the street by the Checker of the Hope, an inn built by Christ Church Priory in 1392. This original building was almost square in plan with a galleried central courtyard and stone arcading on the ground floor along the High Street frontage. The Checker of the Hope contained shops and part of it still survives, especially at the Mercery Lane/High Street corner where the Swatch shop is currently located.

The left hand side of The Checker was destroyed in the fire of 1865 and following the fire many corpses were removed by local volunteers. Some have claimed to hear the cries of those that perished still calling out from the rebuilt frontage on the High Street, and there are 'strange feelings' in the cellars of the properties and at the Sun Hotel, where guests often report they feel they are being moved in their beds.

This could be a great place to stay then if you fancy waking in the night to see a lost soul standing by your bed. Even in recent years, a number of small fires have broken out in the timber framed roofs of properties along the High Street and Butchery Lane, so watch out!

The Old Theatre and Dickens' Ghost

The reason that Charles Dickens came here to Canterbury in 1849 was for a recitation of his new part-work *David Copperfield*, which was partly based on characters he had observed around Canterbury the previous year. Dickens presented this to city dignitaries in what was then the new theatre of Canterbury, located where the entrance to Debenhams' bedding and home-ware department is now.

Dickens' ghost has allegedly been seen here on the ground floor, but since the last sighting the building has changed so greatly it is difficult to find the exact position were you to go in there today. You may feel a bristle of your hackles but more likely it would be the air conditioning units.

The building does, however, house some other ghosts. Many who have worked there over the years claim to have come across one of the store's previous floor managers, dating from the days when it was called Lefebvre's. This was one of the first department stores in the country, then bought by Debenhams in 1973 and converted into the shop you now see. However, 'Old George' as he has come to be known, has been seen by generations of workers on this site. He stands on duty overseeing the workers at the top of the sweeping stairs, which were once the stairs up to the upper dress circle when the building was a Victorian theatre. In what was once the toy department of the old Lefebvre's store on the top floor, many staff have reported seeing out of the corner of their eye objects being moved late at night as they are locking up, and in some cases when they start work the next morning, objects have been balanced in impossible situations.

On one occasion a girl who had set up a large Lego display was surprised to find that overnight the display had been moved so it was about to fall off the edge of a high shelf, when the night before it had been placed safely by the till. The weight of the object meant that it would have taken more than three people to lift it.

The Old
Theatre and
Dickens' Ghost

The Elizabethan Guest Chamber, High Street

This started life as an inn for pilgrims and in 1573 Elizabeth I met a suitor, the Duc d'Alençon, younger brother of Charles XI of France.

Now converted into yet another coffee shop, this once great structure is at least still open to explore, unlike so many of Canterbury's other great buildings. As you go in, look for the Tudor beams above the counter, and at the back near the toilets look out for the old fireplace and a small entrance to a staircase in the far left-hand corner. The original staircase has been removed and replaced with a newer staircase. By now readers may be asking why so many ghosts appear to be seen or felt on staircases, but the reason is simple. While a romantic could say it is a way of 'ascending to a higher plane,' staircases are often the oldest part of a building and are rarely moved or closed, meaning that centuries of humans have climbed up and down.

This building has its fair share of strange sightings; during the building process to convert it into a coffee shop, several strange objects were found on the old stairwell, from a sixteenth-century child's shoe to a collection of thirteenth-century silver coins. They appeared over several weeks, during which time the site was secured each night by the site foreman. Each morning he would make a sweep of the site to make sure it had not been broken into.

The cellars of this old inn also seem to hold a key to its past. Both this building and the one next door, now a Cuban restaurant, were used to house prisoners from the Napoleonic wars, and in the cellars you can still see the remains of the chain holes and cage rests as a vivid reminder of the past.

Some of the coffee shop's staff have felt cold spots inside the building on different floors. I used to finish my ghost tour in the alley alongside and on several occasions, not just on Halloween, the groups often saw the face of a small child tapping at the window located above the middle of the building. Many assumed wrongly she was a resident of the house, but at the time this coffee shop was a fruit shop, with empty rooms above.

The Buttermarket/Olive Branch

The old Buttermarket Inn, formerly known as the Olive Branch, is protected by the Guardian Monk who inhabits the cellar of the pub. There have been several ghost watches here in the past and I have been invited in by some psychics to verify the 'feeling' of an angry man in the cellar.

The Elizabethan Guest Chamber, High Street

The
Buttermarket/
Olive Branch

Many of the old inns of the city had passages linking them to the Cathedral precincts, allowing a steady (and unseen) supply of beer to the clergy, and meaning guests in the inns could pray and worship in the Cathedral outside the official times of worship. The curfew bell – which still rings at around 9 p.m. every evening – was also an important part of daily life in the old city. The rule was that those who were not inside the city walls before the bell chimed would be locked outside, beyond the protection offered by the city guard. In violent times when the rule of law was patchy at best, this must have been a good incentive to get home on time.

Although the pub appears to have an authentic Georgian frontage, it was actually part of a medieval pilgrims' inn called The White Bull, which still extends to the left of the current building. Investigations in the 1960s revealed that the roof spaces of all the buildings were joined and easy access could be had from either side. It was during this investigation that the skeletal remains of a woman were found tied to the crown post in the attic space. She appeared to have died of unnatural causes and the tattered remains of her dress suggest she was a nun, though the reason for her death remains a mystery.

During my last visit to the upstairs rooms, which provides an outstanding view of the square below, I became aware of a vague ghostly outline that could have been a nun. Several of the building's staff had mentioned to me that the building's ghostly resident made their life hard, as 'she' used to throw objects around the kitchen. At first it sounded like the building had a poltergeist, but ghosts do retain the ability to let us know of their presence even if we are unable to see them.

The Old White Bull Inn, Nos 41-42 Burgate

This building, like so many in the city, has been through a variety of uses. Now a retail shop selling cookery items, until a few years ago it was a branch of Laura Ashley. In the 1980s, activity in the attic attracted the attention of the local newspaper.

Stocktaking one night in 1989, the manageress found herself working on the books in a room behind the dormer windows in the attic. Later she claimed to have heard footsteps running across the floor in the room above. Concerned it was an intruder; she grabbed a stepladder and made her way up through the attic hatchway. What she saw chilled her to the bone, and froze her to the top step.

It was dark, but street lights from the square outside illuminated the phantoms of twelve monks standing silently at the far end of the attic toward Burgate Street. Unlike so many ghosts, they seemed acutely aware of the presence of the manager staring blankly at them, yet they made no attempt to flee. Instead they started walking toward her, their footsteps now silent, gliding slowly to her side.

Fearing for her life the manageress descended the ladder at top speed and took cover in her office. She then called her assistant, who climbed the ladder and came back down again at top speed. When she asked what he had seen, he claimed to have seen twelve monks standing at the hatchway praying. They appeared not to see him, but he felt that 'death was around them'.

The incident was reported in the local paper and many local psychics and ghost hunters got involved. The only successful investigation was led by the Dean and Chapter from the Cathedral who sent in an expert from London. He diagnosed this sighting as a simple haunting that was better left alone and the

The Old White
Bull Inn, Nos
41–42 Burgate

result was that the attic was sealed until very recently.

When the loft was reopened, an investigation took place to establish if there was any factual basis for the visitations of so many monks in the attic. The investigation found that the remains of many bones had been found up there in a wooden box, which may well have been the remains of those killed during the English Civil War, when Canterbury was attacked three times by Cromwell's armies.

The Cathedral Gate Hotel, No. 36 Burgate

The Cathedral Gate Hotel, now a Starbucks, was used in the 1942 film *A Canterbury Tale* by Powell and Pressburger to show the devastation caused in

The Cathedral Gate Hotel, No. 36 Burgate

England by the June 1942 German bombings and to reiterate the importance of pulling together for the war effort. Locally the building is still referred to as the 'Cathedral Gate Tea Rooms'. Looking around this great old structure, you are immediately struck by the mass of Tudor bricks that make up the side wall as you enter, and by the mighty oak beams that support the structure above. The building is still part of the Cathedral Gate Hotel, which offers stunning views of the Cathedral, and was always the place to stay if you wanted to be first into the Cathedral in the mornings, since it used to have its own entrance into the precincts. Sadly this entrance is now closed.

Where the gateway now stands was once part of the original Sun Inn, but most of the old Sun Inn was pulled down in 1499 to make way for the new gateway. Local legend has it that the reason the Sun Hotel was built in its current location was as compensation for pulling half the Sun Inn down.

The hotel has had a number of hauntings and sightings; the most commonly reported are those by guests who stay in the rooms on the first and second floors which adjoin the Christchurch Gate itself. Guests often report feeling the presence of something standing by their bed, while others have heard doors slamming late at night when others in the next room have heard nothing when asked about it the following morning.

Most recently singing or ghostly chanting was heard by one of the housekeeping staff, in the early morning as she was preparing the linen for the morning rounds. It came, she said, from behind a wall in the first floor room… In the first floor room there was once a built-in wardrobe. If you walked inside it you could clearly see in the wall the bricks of the edge of Christchurch Gate, for that too is built of brick and faced with stone, making it lighter than it looks.

Timpson's of Canterbury, No. 9 Butchery Lane

Back in 1993, whilst I was working in central Canterbury, there was a famous case of Christina, a young girl who had raised money for charity to stay in an allegedly haunted property in Butchery Lane over Hallowe'en.

Before I go into more detail, here is a little history of Butchery Lane and Slaughterman's Alley. From the Middle Ages until the early twentieth century, Canterbury was a market town famous for cattle trading. The area now called the Buttermarket was once known as the Bull Stake Market, where bulls were tied to a pole in the middle of the square and auctioned off to the town butchers whose stalls and shops were found in Butchery Lane.

After the bulls were traded, they were slaughtered in a place called Slaughterman's Alley, located where the Canterbury Pottery now stands, and

Timpson's of
Canterbury,
No. 9
Butchery Lane

skinned in a place called Skinners Yard, still to be found behind Casey's Pub in Butchery Lane.

The skins of the bulls were then taken to the Williamsons Tannery, now a development of new houses, and turned into leather which the leather-workers of St Dunstan's and Wincheap then transformed into leather goods, like the shoes sold in Long Market Place. The main butchery shop that remains intact today from that era is located behind Timpson's key-cutting shop.

During the English Civil War, a man's body, which had allegedly been skinned alive, was discovered hanging from the slaughterman's hooks in the back of this shop, following a bloody massacre of Catholic townsfolk by Cromwell's troops. The hooks can still be seen hanging from the roof timbers in the rear of the shop. The real problems started after the shop was refurbished following a fire in the City Arms next door. The shop then expanded into the semi-derelict rear of the shop where the body of the man had been found 300 years previously.

Knowing the history of the place would have suggested to me not to go near the place on Hallowe'en, but Christina was still determined, despite having heard the stories about the hooks swinging from the beams and how many of the staff refused to ever go in to that part of the shop.

She was given a lantern and a camp bed and told to stay in the manager's office. Meanwhile, with her approval, Timpson's had rigged up CCTV to cover the event and still have the tapes to show what happened.

Revivals, No. 42 St Peters Street

Later, Christina said it was unnaturally cold, even for the end of October. The tapes showed her shaking on the bed, but it was in fact the bed itself that was shaking, so badly that after ten minutes or so she was physically thrown from the bed to the floor. That was enough for her and she promptly left the building.

Revivals, No. 42 St Peter's Street

This small shop may not attract your attention unless you know some of its history. Like so many properties in this street, it is medieval in construction, but has been extended and re-built over many centuries. Outwardly it has an air of friendliness until, that is, you venture up the back stairs to the upper floors. As you make your way up the narrow winding staircase the temperature drops sharply, even with the central heating on or in the summer. You also feel something is climbing the stairs with you, or as if something is trying to get past you but somehow does not have the energy to do so.

Many psychics have visited the shop and all claim to feel that it is a French soldier. This is quite possible given Canterbury's proximity to the Channel, but also when we consider that it may have been a hiding place for an escaped prisoner of war during the Napoleonic Wars.

Psychics also say that the soldier of France is very angry, but the owner of Revivals has only felt the grim atmosphere for the last ten years, and says it started only after she made a small adjustment to the back window. The soldier seems unhappy about the change. When I went up there some three weeks ago I certainly felt the cold hand of death in that upper room.

Café St Pierre, No. 43 St Peter's Street

When I first came to the city in the mid-1980s this was a sweet shop. The box-throwing poltergeist within first came to my attention when the local paper published a story about the owner at the time.

Mrs Julie Gilmore told the *Kentish Gazette* about the problems she had whilst sleeping in the upstairs rooms. Her first experience came soon after she took over the shop; within the first six weeks she began to feel that, although she was single, she was never alone in the property, and felt unseen eyes were watching her. Occasionally she felt things were hiding in the shadows.

It did not stop there; her shop specialized in chocolates and sweets generally stored in boxes, and on several mornings she awoke to find that her bed covers and bed had been moved several feet whilst she slept.

Café Saint Pierre, No. 43
St Peter's Street

One morning during the summer holidays, she had been looking after her
nephew George while her brother was on holiday. Going to wake up her
nephew, she found that she had inadvertently left a razor blade in the sink in
his room. The child was only four years old at the time, and unable to reach
inside the sink, but she found the sheets of his bed had been shredded. The
boy was awake and unscathed. Her nephew then referred 'to another child
called Daniel in the room' whom she was unable to see, so assumed it was
simply George making up stories. But certain things did not make sense: her
nephew George said that 'Daniel' had referred to an object she kept in the
attic, an attic which she kept locked and which she had never talked about
with little George.

The object in question was an old oak chest given to her by her grandfather several years before, which contained a collection of old papers and some sixteenth century clothes, handed down from a distant relation. Her nephew told her that 'Daniel' had said that he liked playing with the clothes as it reminded him of his childhood. Confused, she ran up the attic stairs to check that the box was intact and found that the padlock had been opened without a key and the clothes were strewn all over the attic space.

Horrified that the building might be haunted, Mrs Gilmore said in a clear voice 'If that is you, Daniel, give me a sign'. At that moment she heard the door to the attic slam closed and the box lid slammed shut. She ran to the door but was unable to open it, and for a moment she thought she was trapped for good. Just as she was about to panic, the jammed door swung open.

She told me recently that nothing more had occurred after that, but her nephew still mentions 'Daniel' at around Christmas time every year.

St Mary Magdalene Church Tower, Burgate

Legend has it that following his execution, the hand of Becket was removed from the man's body by Hue d'Moreville. Fleeing from the scene of the crime he was heading for Sandwich to relay the news to Henry II in France, but as he passed this spot his horse was startled and flung him from his saddle. The fall killed him and he died here on the spot where St Thomas' Church now stands. It has been a Catholic centre of worship since its inception.

D'Moreville allegedly dropped the hand of Becket as he fell from his horse. The hand still bore Thomas a Becket's ring of office, and is now held in the Cathedral Treasury where it can be seen in the permanent exhibition in the Undercroft. After the execution, the remains of Becket's hand were kept in a box that would be kissed by pilgrims.

If you stand beneath the tower on a dark night in December, many locals claim that the night of the murder is replayed on the Burgate. The neighing and clatter of horses' hooves have also been heard on other nights around Christmas and New Year.

Nobody has reported seeing the phantom of D'Moreville since 30 December 1726, when city watchman Edward Denne of Burgate Street claimed in the *Kentish Gazette* that he had seen the figure of a man in very old fashioned clothes on a black horse racing down the Burgate at three o'clock in the morning as he was making his rounds of the city.

The monks who lived and worked in the Whitefriars monastery regularly walked toward the Cathedral on a path that has long been lost beneath the modern streets of the city. Many have seen them still walking the route since the Reformation.

St Mary Magdalene Church Tower, Burgate

The Cherry Tree Pub, White Horse Lane

The Cherry Tree Pub in Whitehorse Lane is a well known haunted location in the city and many people have seen the ghost of the little girl who stands forlorn and lost the outside the pub. 'She' is reputed to date from a time in the late 1920s when the White Horse Hotel, from which the lane gets its name, and the adjoining Fleur de Lys Hotel burned to the ground after The White Horse Hotel caught alight during building work. During the fire a total of twelve people were burned to death as roof beams collapsed, trapping them in the structure. Canterbury's fire wardens did an excellent job of quenching the fire but only two corpses were recovered from the wreckage. The ghosts of some of those who perished now appear, including the spirit of one young girl – a chambermaid who had been working in the upstairs rooms when

The Cherry
Tree Pub,
White Horse
Lane

the roof collapsed, crushing her and three of her colleagues in the burning structure.

Her mother, Ruth Benn, reported seeing her daughter by her side in her garden on the same morning at her home in the village of Old Wives Lees near Chilham, some five miles from the city. She sensed that her daughter was in mortal danger, but there was nothing she could do but wait helplessly until the next day when the Canterbury Constabulary confirmed the death of her thirteen year-old daughter in the fire.

Three students last saw the little girl in 2005 whilst on an evening out from the University of Kent, Canterbury. She was seen standing by the entrance to the car park of the then County Hotel, now the Abode Hotel. On an internet blogging site they described her 'with a silvery sheen surrounding her, with head bowed and hands by her side, walking down White Horse Lane toward the Salvation Army Hall.'

This devastating fire happened during the early spring and left the centre of the city devastated. The owner of the Fleur de Lys Hotel had many bookings for the summer season and hit upon the idea of using the unemployed labour in the city at the time (around the 1929 Depression era) to help him build a new hotel in time for the summer season. The owner had earlier purchased the home of Mary Tourtel in Ivy Lane and that summer decided to use the surrounding land to build his replacement hotel. Now called the Chaucer Hotel, it was constructed in ten weeks and was open in time for the 1929 summer season.

The Chaucer Hotel, No. 63 Ivy Lane

Several sightings have also been reported here. Some months ago I was called late at night by the hotel manager, who was concerned that he had come across the spirit of an elderly woman in the room named after Mary Tourtel, the creator of Rupert Bear.

The Chaucer Hotel has its own ghostly secrets, as does the adjoining building, called Micawbers and currently used as staff accommodation. Several guests staying in one room at the Chaucer have felt unseen fingers stroking them as they sleep, and on one occasion one young girl noticed that the temperature in the hallway was so cold she shivered as she made her way down the corridor toward the main stairs. When she got to the top, she felt a pair of hands on her shoulders and claimed she was pushed hard down the stairs. She managed to stop herself from falling the entire length, but was left with the distinct impression that she herself was the target of the malevolent spirit.

History tells us that Ms Tourtel did in fact die in the room where the hidden hands are felt. One room on the floor above has also unnerved guests, especially when writing appeared on the mirror of the bathroom following a late night shower. The writing was indistinguishable, but had a cursive form to it and appeared to be some kind of name. Often a spirit remains for years to come, but there is nothing violent, apart from the natural death of Ms Tourtel, to be found recorded about the building.

When I worked at the Chaucer Hotel as a waiter in the 1980s there were several strange occurrences in Micawbers, the house next door. Bed sheets were pulled off beds, running footsteps were heard on the stairs and the regular sound of a child crying was heard in the night.

The Chaucer
Hotel, No. 63
Ivy Lane

The House Of Agnes, No. 71 St Dunstan's Street

The site on which the House of Agnes now stands was once a Roman pottery kiln, one of several located along St Dunstan's Street, a safe distance from the city walls. Inside the garden stand two ancient yew trees, a remnant of its previous incarnation as a Roman cemetery. The House of Agnes has been an inn for travellers and pilgrims since the thirteenth century; *The Canterbury Tales* written by Geoffrey Chaucer between 1387-1400 told the story of a group of characters on a pilgrimage from London to the shrine of Thomas a Becket in Canterbury Cathedral. They would have passed the House of Agnes to enter the

The House of Agnes, No. 71 St Dunstan's Street

city through the historic Westgate located just 100m further down the road.

During renovations in 2005, an historic scientific instrument, now known as 'The Canterbury Quadrant', was unearthed at the House of Agnes. It has since been found to be one of only eight still in existence. A flurry of media and scientific interest followed its discovery and it is due to be placed on permanent display at the British Museum from 2009.

The House of Agnes is so called because in the nineteenth century it was the home of Agnes Wickfield, who featured in Charles Dickens' famous novel *David Copperfield*. Several passages in the book describe both the exterior and interior of this historic building, so it is probable that Dickens either stayed here or was very familiar with its interior.

During the late 1990s I used this venue to host the telling of ghost stories by the fireside, when there were some very spooky things going on inside. In one room, at the top of the building overlooking the garden, a guest claimed that the door to his room kept being slammed shut during the night, but when he got up to investigate he found that he had locked it shut before going to bed.

John Durcan, the one time manager of the House of Agnes, recounts how he was locking up late one night when he went to check on the toilets. On the way he heard someone fall over and crash to the floor, but when he went to investigate, he found the toilets were empty and very cold, colder than normal. As he closed the door and put the light out, he heard a cubicle door slam closed. Switching the light back on, he was bemused to see that both cubicle doors were now open. He walked toward the cubicles but as he did so the door slammed closed behind him, and the light bulb flashed and went out. He was left alone in the dark, feeling there was a presence in the room with him, which seemed to push him to one side as it made its way out to the corridor.

Castle House, No. 28 Castle Street

Should you stay at this well known bed and breakfast establishment, you may end up sleeping in the Hangman's Guardroom. If you look from the outside of the building you can see the sunken window, or Hangman's Window, from where the city guard would wave to the crowds to indicate that an execution had taken place. This is because just outside this property, on what is now the roundabout, stands the site of one of the city's original gallows or hanging places. It was also used during the sixteenth-century witch-hunting trials and burnings in Canterbury.

For many years the house was a private residence, but when it was converted to a bed and breakfast establishment, several of the recent guests reported that they had seen the ghostly figure of a sixteenth-century guardsman standing at the foot of their beds, looking out of the window.

Canterbury Castle

The castle stands as testament to the ravages of time. Built by the Normans in 1070, it replaced the earlier Saxon castle with its motte and bailey construction which now lies inside Dane John Gardens. The keep was so well-built that it withstood two sieges by Cromwell's armies in the mid-seventeenth century, but

Castle House,
No. 28 Castle Street

Above and left Canterbury Castle

it eventually fell into disrepair and was later used as a coal store between the two world wars.

The grounds are now tranquil and calm, in stark contrast to the roar of traffic that now seems to haunt the ring road. Late at night after the pubs have closed, local residents have claimed that the spirits of guards are seen wandering around the perimeter walls – perhaps they are the ghosts of those who died defending the city from Oliver Cromwell.

Above and below The White Hart Inn, Worthgate Place

The White Hart Inn, Worthgate Place

During the English Civil War there were so many dead and dying that this pub was used as a dumping ground for the bodies. On one documented occasion the cellar boy was working on tapping the newly arrived barrels when forty corpses were thrown into the cellar, trapping him under them. The spirit of the young boy is regularly felt by the current staff. The cold feeling that is felt before he appears has been commented on by generations of licensees. Many drinkers say they too have felt oppressive feelings as they leave through the old churchyard that adjoins the structure. There appears to be no reason for this to be haunted as all were laid to rest.

Cogan House, No. 53 St Peter's Street

Cogan House is named after John Cogan who lived here in the late 1600s. He was a descendent of the first owner, Luke the Moneyer, who started work on the site in 1180 soon after the death of Thomas a Becket. It was then passed into the hands of William Cokyn who charitably granted it to the Thomas Hospital further down the road. This rich history ensures this building is one of the oldest inhabited buildings in the city, but from the outside it looks simply like a Victorian building, with a modern restaurant inside.

It was during the ownership of Cogan that the first sightings were made in the upper back room, on the left hand side of the room which now looks over the garden. It was said to be a figure clothed in Elizabethan dress, who would rush past anyone who dared enter the room. This appearance was usually followed by a strong gust of wind and often the doors of the upstairs area would slam shut. Late at night, John Cogan's diary claims, he was woken by a man standing by the end of his bed, his hands clasped before him as if in prayer. Cogan claimed that he recognised the face as that of the previous owner of the property, Ralph Bawden, who had died of a fever in 1611 aged just forty-seven. The long hair and forked beard were distinctive features of the man who added the fine plaster ceilings and carved brackets – originally placed on the old jetted frontage, now relocated to the entrance hall.

The wizened face of John Bygg, the owner of the old King's Mill (now demolished) in the fourteenth century, is said to stand at the top of the stairs and occasionally brush past those ascending the stairs. All those that I have recently spoken to claim that they feel a gust of wind when there are no windows open, often accompanied by the strong smell of rotting fish. In the late seventeenth century the skeletal remains of a man were found in a shallow pit at the rear of the garden. At the time it was assumed to be a suicide and yet there are

Cogan House

numerous sightings of a man sitting hunched on the benches that used to be in the school playground that is located at the end of the garden. Many of the children, past and present, claim to have talked to the old man who always seems friendly, yet no adult has ever seen him, which is pretty common as the unquestioning gaze of a child is often more receptive to the spirit world than a knowing adult who refuses to believe their eyes.

St Thomas' Hospital on the East Bridge

Thomas a Becket was murdered on 29 December 1170 in Canterbury Cathedral. Almost immediately, pilgrims came to visit his tomb and the city had to provide accommodation for them. In 1190, Edward Fitzodbold founded a hospital on the bridge in the High Street and Becket's nephew, Ralph, was probably the first Master. The hospital soon became rich, but it fell out of use after some 150 years. It was refounded in 1342 by Archbishop Stratford, and was probably at its peak in the 1380s when Chaucer wrote *The Canterbury Tales*. In Chaucer's words, pilgrims 'from every shire end of England to Canterbury they wend, the holy blissful martyr for to seek'.

St Thomas' Hospital

At this time the Masters were also responsible for maintaining the East Bridge over the river Stour. In the Reformation period, following the rift between Henry VIII and the Church of Rome, monasteries and places of pilgrimage came under government control and many were sold off to the rich. In 1538, the shrine to St Thomas was destroyed and the hospital went into decline, but in 1584 Archbishop Whitgift made reforms which were protected by Act of Parliament. The hospital had thenceforth to provide accommodation for ten poor people of Canterbury and pay dole to ten more. A school for twenty boys had already been founded in 1569, and this stayed open until the 1880s. Today the almshouses remain and are occupied mostly by older persons who have longstanding connections with Canterbury.

The hooded figure of a praying monk has been seen here for over 400 years, making it one of the most seen ghosts of the city. The only problem for visitors is that it tends to be witnessed by the residents and although the under-croft is open in the daytime, most sightings seem to be made at dusk in around October and November. The property was first built in the twelfth century as a pilgrims' chapel on the bridge. It was a belief amongst early Christians that a blessing was required before one could pass over a stretch of water, and although our belief system may have changed over the years, architects until as late as the 1850's still incorporated a chapel close to the start of every major bridge construction. The same can still be seen at Tower Bridge, although the chapel is no longer accessible from street level.

Many psychic people who visit the chapel today feel the bristling of many hands surrounding them, with more recent sightings of a white dog, standing to attention at the foot of the stairs of the upper chamber. It makes no sound but can be seen by many non-psychic people. As recently as three months ago I myself came across it whilst researching for this publication. As I approached, it seemed to be aware of my presence and moved to avoid me as if it knew I was looking at it. I felt the hairs on the back of my neck rise as it came back to look me up and down once more as I left, yet the man seated at the desk next to me seemed to be unaware of its presence, looking right past me to other people descending the stair from the upper chamber.

OTHER HAUNTED LOCATIONS AROUND KENT

If you enjoy a chill down your spine, are sensitive to unseen spirits, or just love a good old ghost story, you'll find plenty to intrigue you all over Kent.

The village of Pluckley, not far from Ashford, still claims to be England's most haunted village – at least twelve confirmed ghosts have been recorded in various locations around Pluckley and they include a monk, a teacher, a coach and horses, a White Lady, a Red Lady and a gypsy watercress seller.

Elvey Farm, Pluckley is the place where Living TV's *Most Haunted* presenters stayed when filming in Pluckley. Elvey Farm is a highly rated seven-room B&B. The owners organise occasional events and weekends including a special Haunted Weekend with a village ghost tour, paranormal investigations and guest psychic.

Around Maidstone, Leeds Castle's favourite phantom is a black dog, a phantom beast that is said to bring bad luck to visitors, while Charlotte, a nineteenth-century servant girl, haunts the nearby Larkfield Priory Hotel.

Nearby Petts Farmhouse was dismantled from Burham village and rebuilt at the Museum of Kent Life in Maidstone. After the rebuild, furniture was moved around in the night. Then a puppy got excited every time he entered the farmhouse, although his lively response suggests the ghost is friendly. It is said to be Rebecca Alexander, a farmer's wife who, in 1912, boarded a pony trap holding her newborn baby in her arms. The pony reared up, throwing mother and child to the ground. The baby was unharmed, but Rebecca died. Since then she haunts the farmhouse looking for her baby.

Bluebell Hill, Maidstone is a notorious stretch of road with less benevolent ghostly tales. There have been numerous reports of drivers hitting people who have vanished before emergency services reach the scene. Be careful when you drive along here in the dark...

On a small island in the Medway at Nettlestead, a bridge appears once every November and a monk can be seen throwing a bound and gagged woman from it.

At Eastwell Manor Hotel, Boughton Lees, Ashford, a White Lady has been seen and strange noises have been heard. A housekeeper is said to have left for good after a frightening experience in one of the rooms.

The ghost of a Second World War airman thumbs a lift to Biggin Hill occasionally. In full wartime flying gear, he has been seen at the crossroads by the Spinning Wheel restaurant in Biggin Hill, trying to get a lift back to the Battle of Britain airfield. Local folklore says he crashed his plane over the ridge at Tatsfield and sometimes, early in the mornings, the sound of his Merlin engine can be heard, even though the sky is clear.

At Old Soar Manor in Plaxtol near Tonbridge, a servant girl who was made pregnant by the family priest of the great house haunts the manor to this day.

The manor is the remains of a medieval knight's hall with a thirteenth-century solar (family quarters). Now owned by the National Trust, it was once owned by the Culpepper family, who loom large in Kentish history and whose men-folk were rumoured to have founded their fortunes as the biggest landowners in Kent and Sussex by marrying all the available heiresses of the day.

It is said that the ghost of a young servant girl called Jenny haunts the house. When Jenny was seventeen in 1775 she was called in to help prepare food for a great Christmas feast. While she was busy in the dairy, the family priest, who had been getting himself into the Christmas spirit, took it upon himself to initiate a nativity of his own. When Jenny's personal advent made itself known as a result, she asked the parson what she should do about it and he told her she should marry her boyfriend – a solution that left poor Jenny so unassured that she fainted, hit her head on the font and drowned in it. When she was found, it was assumed that she had committed suicide and was buried in unconsecrated ground, from which she returns from time to time to haunt the old house.

At West Peckham, according to locals, the village is home to a ghostly highwayman, Jack Diamond. It was here, one Friday the thirteenth that he burnt to death in his cottage, which has born his name, Diamond's Cottage, ever since. His ghost has reputedly been seen here on numerous occasions, but only on that supposedly unluckiest of days, Friday the thirteenth.

Penshurst Place too has its ghosts, while The Bottle House Inn nearby, at Smart's Hill, normally noted for its excellent food, has a lady ghost who is 'felt' rather than seen. At one time, parts of the Bottle House were a shop, a farrier's and a shoemender's, and the rear of the pub was originally a skittle alley which, in November 1865, was given to the church. A small chapel was built and to this day there are two graves in the grounds. A ghost, a lady supposedly called Elisabeth, often makes her presence felt rather than seen.

The town of Royal Tunbridge Wells is rich in ghostly apparitions – from the spooks of the Pantiles to the ghostly children of Rusthall's Beacon Tea Garden, and there are more than twenty ghosts lurking around the Pantiles and on the Common. Local expert, Geoff Butler, leads occasional ghost walks, which can be booked through his gemstone shop in The Pantiles.

The villages around are rich in spirit wanderings too – a headless horseman, probably a cavalier, has been seen thundering down a road in Rusthall, while a young mother haunts the site of her former home in Pembury.

At Hever Castle, near Edenbridge, Anne Boleyn is said to cross the bridge over the river Eden at the castle every Christmas Eve. She is also said to walk the castle on Boxing Day and her doleful love songs, sung in a minor key, can be heard from the room where Henry VIII wooed her.

Another ghost has made itself felt in the northwest corner of the castle. Viscount Astor's housemaids were afraid of the corner and of using the spiral staircase. Others too have felt this fear and complained of a feeling of chill and unease when passing the end of the Long Gallery, as though something unpleasant had happened there.

In the Queen's Chamber, visitors occasionally say, 'There are too many people sewing in the room.' The room is empty, apart from portraits on the wall.

In Henry VIII's room, children don't like the horrible looking man sitting on the chair... but adults don't see him.

In 2006 two members of staff at Hever Castle saw what they thought was a housekeeper in the doorway along the corridor of the Tudor Village; one member of staff particularly liked the crossover 1940s style dress. They realised there were no housekeepers at work at that time and went to investigate, but no one was there.

Bayhall, Pembury, near Royal Tunbridge Wells (now a ruin) was once home to the great Kentish Culpeper family and also to the Duke of Buckingham. An unfortunate lady now haunts it by the name of Anne West.

During the Civil War, the hamlet of Rusthall near Royal Tunbridge Wells was occupied by Cromwell's forces while the Royalists preferred Southborough as a temporary centre. It is this fact, which may well account for an unusual incident which occurred in Hurst Wood, just north of Rusthall, in 1966.

One evening a man walking home along the narrow, now overgrown, path from Broomhill Road heard the sound of horses' hooves and, on turning round, was astonished to see the headless figure of a rider bearing down on him. Up to that moment he had dismissed all tales of ghostly happenings as figments of imagination or the results of excessive drink. But, faced with a horseman wearing the apparel thought at the time to be of a medieval knight, his bravado vanished and he fled.

On later examination of the description of the phantom, the figure could well have been that of a 'cuirassier', a member of Cromwell's troops wearing the normal three-quarter armour of laminated plates. As to the reason why the horseman was headless, we can only suppose. Perhaps the soldier had been killed in a skirmish with a group of Royalists or, as has been suggested, an overhanging branch killed him as he sped through the forest.

Some years ago and only a few yards away from that haunted spot, on the Broomhill Road itself, a couple from Tonbridge, visiting some friends on Christmas Eve, saw the figure of a man standing in a hollow at the side of the road. They were travelling too fast to stop the car in time, and drove so close to the silent spectre that they felt they must have hit it. Shocked and upset by the experience, they searched the area for some time, before being forced to accept that they had hurt and damaged nothing other than their own credulity. Derision from friends hearing of the incident turned to puzzlement when a Rusthall resident named Joe recalled that some seventy years earlier a large house and a cottage had existed at the exact bend in the road where the phantom had been. The buildings had lain empty and derelict for many years before being demolished because 'potential buyers were scared away by the ghost of a man who haunted the place'. Joe claimed that his mother knew the people who lived in the house and they frequently stated that the 'cottage is haunted by a man in a grey suit'. The figure seen by the couple was on the exact spot where the cottage had been.

Around Tonbridge, Ightham Mote is said to be haunted, perhaps by the ghost of the woman whose skeleton was discovered behind a sealed panel by workmen undertaking renovations in 1872. Although the old belief that this haunting was something to do with the Gunpowder Plot can be discounted, it is said that an unearthly chill still hangs about the tower, and has proved resistant even to exorcism.

At Steele's Lane, Meopham, the ghost of a young Parisienne is said to walk. In the aftermath of the defeat of the French Emperor Napoleon at the Battle of

Waterloo in 1815, the British army was sent to occupy Paris. Its task was to keep order while the re-established regime of King Louis XVIII was installed. In the event, the French caused little trouble and the British army did not have much to do.

One soldier there was a private in the Buffs, Kent's premier regiment. With time on his hands, the young man dallied with a Mademoiselle Pinard, promising to marry her in due course. As a result, the pretty young girl surrendered to the soldier rather more of her virtue than was normal in those days.

The regiment eventually left Paris and was sent home to Kent. Believing her lover's promises, Mlle Pinard scraped together enough money to buy a wedding dress and to pay for her fare to Kent.

Arriving in Meopham at the soldier's home, the girl found herself cold-shouldered by the man who no longer had any need for her charms. Distraught and penniless, Mlle Pinard dressed herself in what was supposed to be her wedding dress and hanged herself in Steele's Lane. Her ghost lurks there still, standing quietly by the side of the road on the spot where she died. Her sad death served as a warning. In the nineteenth century many mothers would point to the phantom and admonish their daughters to get their man up the aisle before surrendering to him.

At Tonbridge Castle there is a tale of a ghost, seen only once, that isn't seen at the castle itself, but it seems the castle led to her death. In 1892, an unpopular grocer called Elizabeth Lewis 'who always wore a large hat', went looking for her collie dog, which had wandered off. The dog was her only friend. Elizabeth asked everywhere about her dog, but no one responded because they didn't like her. Eventually she heard her dog whimpering and found it had fallen down a deep hole in the castle, which was undergoing repair at the time. Trying to rescue it, Elizabeth fell in herself. No one heard her screams and eventually both she and her dog died. Two years later, a boat maker swore he had seen Elizabeth, in her large hat, and her dog walking home where they both sat happily under a tree...

At Timberden, near Shoreham, a horrifying ghost has been seen at Mr Howard's house. The owner awoke one night to see a lady in a black dress. There suddenly appeared the ghostly head of an old man, his face blood red. It gently rocked backwards and forwards until it reached the window. Another night he awoke to see a headless body dressed in a red coat with a ruff. This also drifted slowly to the window where it remained for several minutes. The ghost is that of a previous owner, a seventeenth-century clown who went mad and hanged himself from the window with piano wire – hence the ghost's severed head. The 'black lady' who appears with him is believed to be his mourning widow.

At Knole, near Sevenoaks, the famous ghost of the Duchess of Cumberland, Lady Anne Clifford, the unfortunate wife of Richard Sackville, is said to walk the dark avenue of chestnut and oak trees to the north of Knole Gate House. The area she walks was named Duchess Walk after her ghost was seen there several times, always on windy moonless nights. Lady Anne married the 'black sheep' of the family, the third Earl, who plunged into the splendour and vanity of court life and subsequently bankrupted himself.

The ghost of a 'Black Knight' is said to roam the older quarters at Knole whenever a misfortune is about to befall Knole. The Knight may also be seen riding silently on horseback among the leafy shadows.

At Combe Bank, Sundridge, Combe Bank School lies in 350 acres of parkland. It was here that Lady Ferres petitioned her husband for divorce and the steward of the estate was asked to give evidence in the petition. Her husband, the Earl of Ferres, was subsequently arrested for the murder of the steward and hanged at London's Tyburn. Before he died, however, he cursed his wife and wished that she should experience a death more painful than his own. She subsequently married Lord Frederick Campbell and eventually died a very torturous death in a fire in the tower of Combe Bank. All that was found of her in the ruins was the bone of one thumb, which was buried at Combe Bank. The ghost of Lady Frederick Campbell is said to still haunt the ground of the estate.

At Ramhurst, near Leigh, other sightings have been reported. Ramhurst, previously a manor and later a farm, was long reported to boast a headless woman dressed in a grey robe that walked about the estate. The influential Culpepper family owned the property but in 1857 it passed into the hands of a retired Indian Army officer. He and his wife were repeatedly disturbed by mysterious voices, phantom footsteps, the sound of rustling silk and other sounds of someone being present, but there was never any explanation for the strange noises. Once, the brother of the mistress of the house and the cook both heard the mysterious voices at the same time. Thinking it must be his sister calling for help, although it was the middle of the night, the startled man hurriedly grabbed a gun and rushed upstairs, only to find his sister sleeping peacefully. At the bedroom door he met the cook who had also heard voices and had come to see whether she could help her mistress... there was no one else in the house at the time.

At The Chequers in Kemsing, the ghost of an English Civil War Cavalier named William is said to haunt the building. He was hung from a beam in the barn, now part of the pub, after overhearing two Roundhead officers discussing battle plans.

Other titles published by The History Press

Canterbury: History You Can See
MARJORIE LYLE

This detailed history of Canterbury is told through its buildings from its Roman origins to the present day. The reader is introduced to the builders, traders, craftsmen and saints and sinners who created Canterbury during its long history and tells many surprising stories about the people behind the buildings creating an informative and entertaining read rather than a text-book history.

978 0 7524 4538 0

Haunted Kent
JANET CAMERON

Haunted Kent contains spooky stories from around the county, including the hunchbacked monk at Boughton Malherbe and the well-known tale of Lady Blanche of Rochester Castle. This fascinating collection of strange sightings and happenings in the county's streets, churches, public houses and country lanes is sure to appeal to anyone wanting to know why Kent is known as the most haunted county in England.

978 0 7524 3605 0

Ramsgate Then & Now
VINCENT RUNACRE

In this book Ramsgate's busy maritime centre, seafront and stunning architecture have been captured in a myriad of images depicting scenes of yesteryear along with contrasting images of contemporary views from over 100 years later. As well as delighting the many tourists who have visited the town over the years, *Ramsgate Then & Now* will provide present occupants with an insight of how the town used to be.

978 0 7524 4458 1

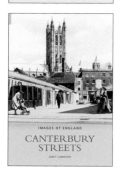

Canterbury Streets
JANET CAMERON

This book examines the streets of Canterbury in an attempt to detail the history of the people and places contained within them and create a sense of the past here. Discover the derivation of the old streets' names, how they have changed and the new routes in this many-layered city. *Canterbury Streets* will delight those who know the area as it was and those who live in the city today.

978 0 7524 3398 1

Visit our website and discover thousands of other History Press books.
www.thehistorypress.co.uk